First Certificate
Writing

Judy Copage

CONTENTS MAP

UNIT	Writing skills	Language area	Vocabulary development
INFORMAL LETTERS			
1 Making contact and giving news, p.4 Describing a language school	Greetings and endings Introductions: personal greetings Introduction to paragraphing Conclusions: sending wishes, etc.	Error correction: typical language errors	Adjectives to describe aspects of school
2 Giving advice, p.8 The best place for a holiday	Recognising the right level of formality Planning paragraphs: topics and relevant details Topic sentences	Giving advice	Clothes and equipment for taking on holiday
3 Describing an object, p.12 Choosing between a stereo and a computer	Paragraphing: grouping information Topic sentences Making an outline: completing a table	Order of adjectives Connectors of reason and result Tenses	Adjectives to describe possessions
FORMAL LETTERS			
4 A letter of application, p.16 Applying for a job in tourism	Greetings and endings Introductions: stating the reason for writing Using the right level of formality Making an outline: completing a table	Relative clauses	Formal and informal vocabulary
5 Making a request, p.20 Returning lost property	Making an outline: completing a table Topic sentences and relevant details	Thanking Polite requests	Word-building: adjective to noun
6 A letter to the editor, p.24 Expressing an opinion on traffic problems	Making an outline: using an ideas map Introductions: stating the topic and your opinion	Expressing opinions Second conditional Connectors of sequence	Traffic and traffic problems
TRANSACTIONAL LETTERS			
7 Asking for information, p.28 A holiday	Analysing the input in the exam question Review of greetings and endings Making an outline: completing a table Paragraphing: grouping and ordering information Introductions: giving background and stating the reason for writing	Indirect questions	Places to stay, hotel facilities and holiday activities
8 Giving information, p.34 Travel arrangements	Summarising the input in the exam question Ordering paragraphs in a model text Topic sentences	Connectors for expressing options Future possibilities	Error correction: typical vocabulary errors
9 Giving and asking for information, p.40 Improving your English	Evaluating two model texts Editing a text	Question formation	Aspects of learning English
10 Making arrangements, p.44 A guest speaker at school	Making a plan Evaluating two model texts Introductions: thanking Conclusions: offering further help and information	Gerunds and infinitives	Prepositions
11 Making a complaint, p.50 A disappointing weekend break	Evaluating style and tone Paragraphing: writing main paragraphs Introductions: giving background and stating the reason for writing Conclusions: requesting action to be taken	Connectors of contrast and addition Reported speech	Adjectives to describe feelings *-ing/-ed* adjectives
STORIES			
12 Describing an accident, p.56	Making an outline: completing a table Writing an effective introduction	Narrative tenses	Vocabulary to create a vivid picture
13 Describing an event, p.60 A wedding	Evaluating two model texts	Non-defining relative clauses	Weddings

14	A journey, p.64 A journey in bad weather	Making an outline: completing a table Introductions: setting the scene	Narrative tenses Connectors of concession	Weather conditions and effects of bad weather
15	A story beginning, p.68 My first time on stage	Paragraphing Guided writing from notes	Connectors of time Future in the Past	Performing and being on stage
16	A story ending, p.72	Selecting a topic for an open-ended question Paragraphing and linking Editing a text	Punctuation of direct speech	Adjectives to describe emotions Reporting verbs

DISCURSIVE COMPOSITIONS

17	Discussing pros and cons, p.76 Taking exams	Identifying different kinds of discursive questions Making an outline: completing a table Introductions: stating the general topic Conclusions: giving a balanced personal comment	Connectors of sequence, contrast, addition and result The definite article	Words to express positive and negative aspects of a topic
18	Giving your opinion (1), p.80 School subjects	Analysing a model text Paragraphing: analysing structure	Connectors of result Expressing opinions	School subjects Practical skills
19	Giving your opinion (2), p.84 Young people and their leisure time	Analysing a model text Guided writing: gapped composition Paragraphing: organising information and linking	Connectors of exemplification	Sports and outdoor activities go, do and play
20	Suggesting solutions, p.88 Endangered species	Paraphrasing the language in the exam question Evaluating two model texts Introductions: giving background and stating the overall topic Revising a poor model Editing a text	Language errors in text	Endangered species

REPORTS

21	Evaluating places, p.92 A new tourist attraction	Report format and style Making a plan Introductions: stating the purpose of the report Conclusions: making a recommendation	Passives	Formal and informal vocabulary
22	Evaluating proposals, p.96 A stadium or a theatre	Report format Writing headings in a report Making an outline: completing a table	Second conditional	make and do
23	Suggesting improvements, p.100 Improving a museum	Evaluating a model text	Formal, polite suggestions	Word-building

ARTICLES

24	Describing people and relationships, p.104 Notable people	Analysing a model text Selecting background and main information	Connectors of reason	Qualities of notable people Word-building
25	Reviewing, p.108 Favourite TV programmes	Analysing a model text Making a plan	Superlatives and Present Perfect	TV programmes Adjectives of similar meaning
26	Language learning, p.112 How to improve your speaking	Selecting an appropriate style Analysing a model text Introductions: getting the reader's attention Making a plan	Inversion for emphasis	Collocation: verbs and nouns

SET BOOK ESSAYS

27	Discussing the plot, p.116	Making notes on set books Paragraphing Making an outline: completing a table	Present tenses for summarising events in a set book	Vocabulary to discuss literature
28	Discussing characters, p.120	Making and organising notes on characters Planning content with reference to set books Evaluating a model text Revising a poor model	Improving language in a model text	Adjectives to describe characters

Writing Bank, p.124

Informal letters

1 Making contact and giving news

1 Read the question

In both parts of Paper 2 of the exam, there are questions which ask you to write a letter. In Part 2 of the exam, you may be asked to write a letter to a friend in which you make contact and give news. **Read the exam question below and underline the key words. Use the questions which follow to help you.**

> You are studying abroad in an English-speaking country. Write a letter to your pen friend, describing the school and saying what you like most **and** what you like least about the school.

Write your **letter**, describing your school (120–180 words). Do not write any addresses.

1 Where are you when you write your letter?

2 What are you doing there?

3 Who are you writing to?

4 How many topics are there in the question?

5 What should you write about in your letter?

   a the positive things

   b the negative things

   c the positive and the negative things

<table>
<tr><td>exam tip</td></tr>
<tr><td>When you read the question, you must identify the key words first, before you start to write. You should always underline these words and keep looking back at the question as you plan your answer.</td></tr>
</table>

2 Think about your reader

Work with a partner. Look at the exam question again and answer the following questions.

1 Who is going to read your letter?

   a a friend you know well

   b a member of your family

   c a person you have never met

   d your boss, or your teacher

2 Why are you writing the letter?

   a to ask for information

   b to give advice

   c to give news

   d to ask for help

3 What style of writing should you use?

   a formal

   b informal

4 Which of the following greetings and endings are suitable for your letter?

   a Dear friend, … Love, Olga

   b Dear Anna, … Love, Olga

   c Dear Anna, … Yours sincerely, Olga

   d Dear pen friend, … Yours sincerely, Olga

3 Brainstorm the topic

Work with a partner. Imagine you are at a language school in Britain. What would the following aspects of the school be like?

- the location
- your classmates
- your teachers
- the classrooms
- the lessons
- the facilities

<table>
<tr><td>tip</td></tr>
<tr><td>When you write, try to use your personal experience wherever possible. If the topic is unfamiliar to you, ask yourself:
<ul>
<li>Have I done something similar?</li>
<li>Have I heard someone else talk about it?</li>
<li>Have I seen something on TV about it?</li>
<li>Have I read about it?</li>
</ul>
This will save you time in the exam.</td></tr>
</table>

4 Think about vocabulary

a Work with a partner. Think about the school where you study English, or a school you have attended in another country. Make notes about the good and bad points of the school. Organise your notes into topics in the table below.

Topic	Positive	Negative
Building/Classrooms	*brightly painted*	*cramped classrooms*
Classmates		
Teachers		
Lessons		
Facilities		
Location		

b Write sentences with the words and phrases in the box below and the topics from column 1 of the table. Some words and phrases can go with more than one topic., e.g. *interesting* can describe lessons, teachers and classmates.

> **boring brightly decorated cramped demanding depressing disorganised encouraging friendly fun funny gloomy helpful interesting long kind motivating noisy spacious stimulating strict well organised**

5 Think about your introduction

a Read the introduction to the model text on p.6 and underline the expression Olga uses to greet her friend. What other expressions of this type can you think of? (See **Writing Bank**, p.124.)

b What else does Olga say in her introduction?

c Now write an introduction for the following letters.

1 Your pen friend has just written you a long letter, giving you all his/her news.

2 You haven't written to your pen friend for a long time, because you have had exams at school.

6 Think about paragraphing

Read the following extracts from a letter. Which one is easier to read? Why?

tip

When you write an informal letter, you should begin by greeting your friend and giving some recent news in your introduction.

1

The school is well organised and the classrooms are very spacious. The teachers are very demanding and I have too much homework to do! The cafeteria sells terrible food, but my classmates are from many different countries and are very friendly. We have a lot of fun together. The chairs are very uncomfortable in the class, but the teachers are motivating and encouraging, so I'm learning a lot! The school is on a busy street, so the noise is a problem sometimes.

2

The school is well organised, and the classrooms are very spacious. The teachers are encouraging and motivating, so I'm learning a lot. My classmates are from many different countries and are friendly. We have a lot of fun together.

There are a few things I don't like. Sometimes the teachers are very demanding and I have a lot of homework to do. The school is on a busy street, so noise is a problem. Also, the chairs are very uncomfortable, and the cafeteria sells terrible food!

1 Making contact and giving news

7 Read a model text

Read the model text below. The introduction and the conclusion are in the correct order, but the sentences in paragraphs 2 and 3 have been mixed up. Number the sentences in the correct order, and then decide where paragraph 3 begins.

Dear Anna,
    How are you? I'm sorry I haven't written for so long, but I was very busy getting ready to come to England for my summer English course.

a The chairs are very uncomfortable, too!

b The teachers are encouraging and the lessons are great fun!

c Unfortunately, not everything is good.

d I arrived last week, and I'm really enjoying myself, because the school is so well organised and friendly.

e The worst thing is that the classrooms are very cramped and dark, so they're rather depressing.

f I also really like my classmates, who are from all over the world, and it's really interesting learning about their countries.

g It doesn't really matter, though, because I enjoy practising my English and being in a foreign country.

    I would really like you to visit me this summer. Write to me and tell me your plans.
                                        Love,
                                        Olga

tip

When you write, make sure you use one paragraph for one topic. If you are writing about the good points and the bad points of a topic, make sure you have all the good points in one paragraph, and all the bad points in another.

8 Think about your conclusion

a Look back at the model text on p.6. What does Olga do in the conclusion of her letter to Anna?

b You can finish an informal letter in many different ways. Complete the following conclusions with a suitable word or words. (Sometimes more than one answer is possible.)

1
> Thanks for (1) .... me such a nice birthday card. Please (2) .... to me again soon, and (3) .... me all your (4) ....

2
> Please (1) .... my regards to your (2) ...., and (3) .... and tell me your plans for (4) ....

3
> I would really (1) .... to see you. Why don't you (2) .... and visit me this summer? Write (3) ....!

9 Think about language

All the following sentences contain errors. Find the errors and correct them.

1 I'm sorry I didn't write to you for a long time.

2 I'm very interesting to hear all your news.

3 I'm looking forward to see you soon.

4 Please tell to me everything you did on your holiday.

5 I'll send you a postcard when I'll arrive in Disneyland.

6 When you went to the USA, what have you seen there?

7 I'm waiting to hear from you for a long time.

8 I arrived at London last night.

Exam practice: Write a letter

You are going to write a letter on the topic below. Do the tasks which follow.

> You recently spent a holiday abroad. Write a letter to your pen friend, describing the things you enjoyed the most, **and** the things you enjoyed the least about your holiday.

Write your **letter**, describing your holiday (120–180 words). Do not write any addresses.

● **Read the question**

Underline the key words and answer the following questions.

1 How many topics are there in the question?

2 What are the key points of the topic(s)?

3 What is the situation? Where are you?

● **Think about your reader**

Who is going to read the letter? What style of writing should you use?

● **Think about paragraphing**

To write a letter which is clear for the reader, make sure your letter has:

1 an introduction, greeting and giving news

2 the key points in suitable paragraphs

3 a conclusion

● **Edit your text**

Check your writing for errors when you have finished.

Further practice

Write a letter on the topic below.

> You have a summer job, working in an English-speaking country. Write a letter to your pen friend, describing the job and saying what you like most **and** what you like least about the job.

Write your **letter**, describing your job (120–180 words). Do not write any addresses.

2 Giving advice

1 Read the question

In Part 2 of the exam, you may be asked to write a letter to a friend in which you give advice. **Read the exam question below and underline the key words. Use the questions which follow to help you.**

> Your English pen friend wants to visit your country and has written to you for advice and information. Write a letter to your pen friend, giving advice about the best place to spend a holiday **and** telling him or her what clothes and other equipment to pack.

Write your **letter**, giving advice to your pen friend (120–180 words).
Do not write any addresses.

1 Are you going to write a new letter, or reply to one?

2 What are the two topics you have to write about in your letter?

2 Think about your reader

Work with a partner. Look at the exam question again and answer the following questions. (Sometimes more than one answer is possible.)

1 Who is going to read your letter?

2 What does your reader want to know?

    a information about what to pack

    b your opinion on the best place to visit

    c information about buying tickets

    d information about how to travel

    e reasons why it is a good place to visit

    f a description of your last holiday

3 Which of the following extracts is written in the correct style?

a
> In reply to your letter of 15th May, I am pleased to advise you on the best place for your holiday.

b
> If you want to have a really great seaside holiday, why don't you try my favourite resort?

c
> The White Mountain Resort is my personal recommendation for an enjoyable skiing holiday.

d
> If I were you, I'd rent a motorbike and travel around the countryside. It's great fun!

3 Brainstorm the topic

Work with a partner, answer the questions and make notes.

1 Think of all the places you have been to on holiday in your country. Which place do you think was the best?

2 Where exactly did you go? e.g. *a city with many historical sights, a seaside resort, a village in the mountains*, etc.

3 Why was it the best place? e.g. *It's a place where you can meet young people. There are good entertainment facilities*, etc.

4 When you went on holiday, what did you pack?

4 Think about vocabulary

a Look back at the notes you made in **3 Brainstorm the topic** and add them to the second column of the table below.

Places	Reasons why places are good	Clothes and equipment
Seaside		
Mountains		
City		
Countryside		

b Match the words in the box to the clothes and equipment in the picture. Add these words to the third column of the table in **a**.

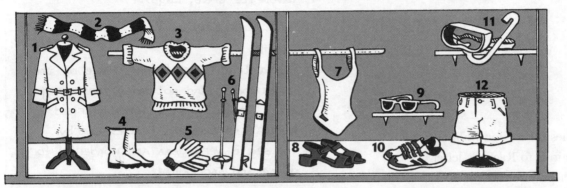

| boots | gloves | raincoat | sandals | scarf | shorts | skis | snorkel and mask |
| sunglasses | sweater | swimsuit | trainers |

5 Read a model text

Read the following letter. Which of the things in **2 Think about your reader** question 2 are included?

Dear Rachel,

Thanks for your letter! It was great to hear all your news. I was very happy to read that you wanted to visit Portugal this summer.

If you want to have a relaxing holiday by the sea, I would recommend my favourite place, Lagos. It's a traditional fishing village on the south coast, and not many tourists go there. It has many reasonably-priced hotels, and excellent beaches nearby. The sea is very clean and wonderful for diving and snorkelling.

You asked me about what clothes and equipment to bring. If I were you, I would pack very little – a swimsuit, and some T-shirts and shorts for the beach. It may get a little cool at night, so bring a sweater, too. Don't forget your snorkel and mask for diving and a ball for playing with on the beach. My advice is to travel light, so you can fill your suitcase with souvenirs to remind you of Portugal!

I hope that you'll enjoy yourself in Lagos. If you want to know anything else, just drop me a line.

Best wishes,
José

6 Think about paragraphing

a Look back at the model text on p.9. How many paragraphs are there?

b Which topics belong in each paragraph? Look at the topics below (a–i) and complete the outline of the letter in the table.

Paragraph	Topics
1	
2	
3	
4	

a wishes for a good holiday

b reactions to Rachel's letter

c description of the place

d offer of help

e advice about clothes

f greetings

g the place recommended

h reasons why it is a good place

i advice about equipment

c Think of another place in your country you can recommend to a pen friend for a holiday. Make notes on:

- the name of the place
- a brief description of the place
- the reasons why you recommend it
- the clothes and equipment your friend would need

d Make an outline for a letter from the notes you made in **c**, following the example in **b**.

exam tip

Remember you have 45 minutes to write your answer. Spend about 15 minutes on getting ideas and writing an outline. You can spend about 20 minutes on writing the answer. Always leave enough time to check your work when you finish writing. Spend about 10 minutes on this.

7 Think about topic sentences

a Look at the first sentence of paragraphs 2 and 3 of the model text on p.9. These are topic sentences, where the writer makes a general statement about the main topic of the paragraph. Then there are details to explain and support the topic sentence.

Topic sentence

If you want to have a relaxing holiday by the sea, I would recommend my favourite place, Lagos.

Details

It's a traditional fishing village on the south coast, and not many tourists go there. It has many reasonably-priced hotels, and excellent beaches nearby. The sea is very clean and wonderful for diving and snorkelling.

b Underline the topic sentences in the following paragraphs. How many details are there in each paragraph?

1

The west coast of Scotland is a wonderful place. There are isolated beaches, where you can be alone all day. The sunsets are quite amazing, too. The scenery is quite breathtaking, and the people are friendly.

2

You asked me what you should pack. It's a good idea to bring a pair of walking boots, and a raincoat. The weather can be very unpredictable! Don't forget your camera — the scenery is so beautiful, and perfect for photography.

c Look back at the outline you made in **6 Think about paragraphing d**. Write a topic sentence for each paragraph you have planned.

8 Think about language
Giving advice

a Look at the following sentences from the model text on p.9. Underline the expressions which give advice.

If you want to have a relaxing holiday by the sea, I would recommend my favourite place, Lagos.

If I were you, I would pack very little …

My advice is to travel light, …

> **More useful phrases for giving advice**
> It would be a good idea to …
> You should/shouldn't …
> Don't forget to …

b Write the following advice to tourists as complete sentences. Use the expressions in **a**.

e.g. bring/umbrella/rain/a lot

If I were you, I would bring an umbrella, because it rains a lot.

1 bring/plenty/suntan lotion/sun/strong

....

....

2 avoid/Mykonos/very crowded/expensive

....

....

3 good restaurant/Chez Michel

....

....

4 stay/guesthouse/very clean/good value for money

....

....

5 exciting nightlife/Club Copacabana

....

....

6 see all the coastline/hire/boat

....

....

7 not visit/August/weather too hot

....

....

8 travel by taxi/buses too slow/unreliable

....

....

Exam practice: Write a letter

You are going to write a letter on the topic below. Do the tasks which follow.

This is part of a letter you have received from a pen friend:

> As part of my studies, I have to write about places of historical interest in a foreign country. When I come to stay with you, I'd like to visit some important historical sights. What do you think are the best places to see? How many places do you think I can visit in 10 days?

Write a **letter**, giving advice to your pen friend (120–180 words). Do not write any addresses.

- **Read the question**
  Underline the key words and identify your reader.

- **Think about paragraphing**
  Make an outline for your letter, with a suitable introduction and conclusion, as well as the main paragraphs.

- **Think about topic sentences**
  Write a topic sentence for each main paragraph.

- **Think about language**
  Choose appropriate phrases to give advice in your letter.

- **Edit your text**
  Check your writing for errors when you have finished.

Further practice

Write a letter on the topic below.

This is part of a letter you have received from your English pen friend:

> Now that I have finished my exams, I want to try and lose some weight. You said in your letter that you had lost over 10 kilos! How did you do it? What do you think I should do to lose weight?

Write a **letter**, giving advice to your pen friend (120–180 words). Do not write any addresses.

Informal letters

3 Describing an object

1 Read the question

In Part 2 of the exam, you may be asked to write a description. In this unit, you will learn how to describe an object in an informal letter. **Read the exam question below and underline the key words. Use the questions which follow to help you.**

This is part of a letter you have received from an English pen friend:

> In your last letter, you said you were going to buy either a new stereo or a new computer. Which did you decide to buy? What's it like? Are you pleased with it? I'd love to hear all about it, and your other news.

Write your **letter**, answering your friend's questions and giving relevant details (120–180 words). Do not write any addresses.

1 Are you going to write a new letter, or reply to one?

2 What are the two choices of topic for your letter?

3 What do you have to write about the topic you choose?
Tick (✓) the correct answers from the following list.

 a a description of the object

 b a comparison of stereos and computers

 c your decision about what you bought

 d the advantages and disadvantages of computers

 e your feelings about your new purchase

4 What else must you include in your letter?

2 Think about your reader

Work with a partner. Look at the exam question again. Which of the following letters should you write? Think about who you are writing to, and what your reader wants to know.

 a a formal letter, giving information

 b an informal letter, describing and giving news

 c an informal letter, inviting and giving news

 d a formal letter, making arrangements

 e an informal letter, giving advice

3 Brainstorm the topic

Work with a partner and answer the questions.

1 Have you got a computer or a stereo? Describe it to your partner.
Think about the following aspects:
- make
- cost
- design
- your opinion
- how you felt when you bought it
- how it has changed your life

2 If you had some extra money, which would you buy, a computer or a stereo? Why?

3 In the exam question, you have to give your pen friend your news. Imagine you haven't seen your friend for a few months. What have you been doing recently? Tell your partner all your news.

4 Think about vocabulary

a Think about your and your family's possessions. Make notes about them in the table below.

Object	Make	Adjectives	Features
Car	*Ford*	*comfortable, blue, large*	*electric windows, air-conditioning*
TV			
Stereo			
Bicycle			
Motorbike			
Computer			
Trainers			
Watch			
Other			

b Write sentences with the adjectives in the box below and the objects from column 1 of the table. Some adjectives can go with more than one object, e.g. *portable* can describe a computer, TV and stereo.

> **bulky   compact   economical   efficient   fashionable   high-tech   luxurious
> portable   reliable   roomy   smart   state-of-the-art   stylish   trendy
> upmarket   user friendly**

c Use the notes you made in **a** to write sentences describing your possessions. (See **Writing Bank**, p.124.)

5 Read a model text

a Read the model text. Has the writer grouped the topics into clear paragraphs? Check the paragraph topics in the first column of the table on p.14.

b Find the topic sentences of paragraphs 1–4 in the model text. Write them in the table on p.14.

c Underline all the ideas in the model text that belong in paragraph 2. Add these ideas to column 3 of the table in note form.

d Put a circle round all the ideas that belong to paragraph 3. Add these ideas to column 3 of the table in note form.

e Rewrite paragraphs 2 and 3, with the correct ideas together.

Dear Sarah,

Thanks for your letter. I'm sorry I haven't written before, but because I have been doing a lot of studying recently, I haven't had time for anything else!

Now for my news. I finally decided on a new computer rather than a stereo. It also makes writing assignments a much shorter task, as I can easily change anything I write. I went on a short trip to visit my grandmother last week. I always enjoy seeing her because we spend hours chatting and gossiping. When I got home, I found that my parents had bought me some new bedroom furniture, so I spent Saturday rearranging my room. The computer was a real bargain and it has made such a difference to my life!

It's a portable, compact notebook which weighs only two kilos; as a result, I can work just about anywhere! I also went to a great beach party, where we had a barbecue and went swimming at midnight!

That's all for now. Write soon, and tell me everything you've been up to recently.

Love,
Nadia

3 Describing an object

Paragraph	First/Topic sentence	Details
1 Introduction Thanks for letter Apologise late reply		
2 Recent news		
3 Bought a computer or stereo Description + benefits Price Feelings		
4 Conclusion Write soon, give news		

6 Think about connectors

a Look at the sentences from the model text on p.13. Underline the words and expressions which show (a) a reason, and (b) a result.

… because I have been doing a lot of studying recently, I haven't had time for anything else!

It also makes writing assignments a much shorter task, as I can easily change anything I write.

When I got home, I found that my parents had bought me some new bedroom furniture, so I spent Saturday rearranging my room.

It's a portable, compact notebook which weighs only two kilos; as a result, I can work just about anywhere!

b Join the following pairs of sentences, using a linking word or phrase of reason or result.

1 I bought a new stereo. My old one was beyond repair.

....

2 I went to my grandmother's house. I hadn't seen her for ages.

....

3 I decided to buy a computer. I finish my homework in half the time.

....

4 I watched TV all night. I was too tired to do well in my exam.

....

5 I spent hours on the Internet. My phone bill was huge!

....

6 I bought a new bicycle. I couldn't stand travelling by bus.

....

7 Think about tenses

a Look at the sentences from the model text on p.13. Underline the verb(s) in each one.

1 … I haven't written before.

2 … it has made such a difference to my life!

3 I went on a short trip to visit my grandmother last week.

4 I always enjoy seeing her …

5 …, I found that my parents had bought me some new bedroom furniture, …

6 I also went to a great beach party, …

b Match sentences (1–6) from **a** with the descriptions (a–d).

  a The Past Perfect is used to express an action which happened before another action in the past.

  b The Present Simple is used to express something which happens repeatedly or is generally true.

  c The Past Simple is used to express an action which happened at a definite time in the past (mentioned or understood).

  d The Present Perfect is used to express a past action when the time of the action is not known or is not important. The past action often has a present result.

c Complete the following text with the correct form of the verb in brackets.

Thanks for your letter. I (1) .... (not write) for a long time because I (2) .... (go) on a school trip last month. It (3) .... (start) with a disaster! When we arrived, we found that all our luggage (4) .... (leave) behind! It (5) .... (arrive) the next day, luckily. (6) .... you ever .... (go) to Paris? It's the most romantic city I (7) .... (ever visit). We (8) .... (go) to great restaurants, and (9) .... (take) crazy photos beside the Eiffel Tower! I (10) .... (never have) so much fun!

Exam practice: Write a letter

You are going to write a letter on the topic below. Do the tasks which follow.

This is part of a letter you have received from an English pen friend:

> As I haven't heard from you for ages, I thought I'd write and ask you your news. What have you been doing? You said you were going to buy a new TV, or a new bicycle. What did you buy? Why? What's it like? I'd love to hear all about it.

Write your **letter**, answering your friend's questions and giving relevant details (120–180 words). Do not write any addresses.

- **Read the question**

  Underline the key words and identify your reader.

- **Think about paragraphing**

  Make an outline for your letter.

- **Think about connectors**

  Use some of the connectors on p.14 to link your text.

- **Think about tenses**

  Use the correct tenses to describe the object and talk about your news.

- **Edit your text**

  Check your writing for errors when you have finished.

Further practice

Write a letter on the topic below.

This is part of a letter you have received from an English pen friend:

> Thanks for your letter. I'm sorry I haven't written for ages, but I've been very busy. By the way, congratulations on winning the school story competition! What did you decide to spend the prize money on? Tell me what you bought, and why. Are you pleased with it? Don't forget to tell me all your other news as well.

Write your **letter**, answering your friend's questions and giving relevant details (120–180 words). Do not write any addresses.

4 A letter of application

1 Read the question

In Part 2 of the exam, you may also be asked to write a formal letter of application for a job, a scholarship, a free offer, etc. **Read the exam question below and underline the key words.**

You have just read the following advertisement in a newspaper:

ENGLISH-SPEAKERS WANTED

We are looking for people to work as information officers in our Central Tourist Office, answering questions and giving information to foreign visitors. Part-time work only, evenings and weekends.

- Do you speak any foreign languages?
- Do you know your country well?
- Do you like meeting people?

Apply in writing to the Director, Central Tourist Office

Write your **letter of application** to the Central Tourist Office (120–180 words). Say why you think you could do the job well. Do not write any addresses.

2 Think about your reader

Work with a partner. Look at the exam question again and answer the following questions.

1 Do you know the name of the person you are writing to?

2 Have you ever met this person?

3 Is your letter for business, or giving news?

4 Which of the following topics would your reader expect to find in your letter?

   a your age

   b your present occupation

   c your previous experience in this kind of job

   d where you live

   e other countries you have visited

   f where you saw the advertisement

   g how much money you expect to earn

   h information about how to contact you

   i what languages you speak

5 Which of the following greetings and endings are suitable for your letter?

   a Dear Sir/Madam, ... Yours faithfully, Simon Garrett

   b Dear Central Tourist Office, ... Yours faithfully, Simon Garrett

   c Dear Sir/Madam, ... Yours sincerely, Simon Garrett

3 Brainstorm the topic

Work with a partner and answer the questions.

1 What kind of person might apply for this job?

e.g. *a university student, a retired person*

2 What skills or knowledge might he/she need?

e.g. *the ability to speak foreign languages, a good knowledge of local places*

3 A good candidate for this job would have to be:

e.g. *friendly, patient*

4 Compare two model texts

a Read the two letters below and answer the following questions.

1 Which letter has the correct greeting and ending?

2 Which letter uses contracted verb forms? Which uses full verb forms?

3 Which letter has a personal tone?

4 Which letter uses impersonal, polite language?

5 Which letter uses informal, conversational vocabulary?

> **tip**
>
> In every formal letter, you must begin by saying *why* you are writing the letter.

Letter A

Dear Central Tourist Office,

I've just read your ad for an information officer in 'The Daily News', and I'm looking for a summer job. This one would be just great!

I'm 20 years old and I'm a student at university. I'm studying French and English, so I think that these two languages could come in handy for talking to tourists, and besides I need the practice! I also had a fantastic holiday in Italy last year, and picked up quite a bit of Italian.

I had a good time last year, working as a tourist guide, so I've got a good knowledge of the city, and I love working with people. In fact, I'm hoping to do a tourism course when I finish college, so I can work in a hotel.

I hope you think I would be OK for the job. Drop me a line or give me a call on 664 9862.

Regards,
Simon

Letter B

Dear Sir/Madam,

I am writing to apply for the job of information officer, which was advertised in 'The Daily News'.

I am 20 years old, and I am studying French and English at university. I have just completed my second year, and would like the opportunity to practise my languages with foreigners. I also speak some Italian. I would also like to gain some valuable experience working with tourists, as I am considering a career in the hotel business when I graduate.

I have always been interested in working with people. I worked as a guide last summer with Blue Sky Holidays, which I enjoyed very much. Because I was working as a guide, I had to study and remember a lot of information, so I would say I have a good knowledge of history, places of interest, and tourist resorts.

I can be contacted at the above address, or by telephone on 664 9862. I look forward to your reply.

Yours faithfully,
Simon Garrett
Simon Garrett

b Which letter will have a more positive effect on the employer because of the way it is written?

4 A letter of application

5 Think about style

a Look at the following extracts from **Letter A**. Read **Letter B** on p.17 and underline the more formal way to express these ideas.

1 I've just read your ad for an information officer in 'The Daily News', and I'm looking for a summer job. This one would be just great!

2 … and besides I need the practice!

3 I also had a fantastic holiday in Italy last year, and picked up quite a bit of Italian.

4 I had a good time last year, working as a tourist guide, …

5 … so I've got a good knowledge of the city, …

6 I hope you think I would be OK for the job. Drop me a line or give me a call on 664 9862.

7 Regards, Simon

b Look at the following list of informal words and phrases. Then look at **Letter B** and find the formal words and phrases that mean the same.

1 finished

2 chance

3 get

4 useful

5 thinking about

6 I know a lot about …

7 Get in touch with me …

8 Write back soon.

c Rewrite the following sentences to make them more appropriate for a formal letter. Change the words in *italics*, using the words and phrases in the box. Make any necessary changes.

1 I *got* my diploma last year.

2 It was *fun*!

3 I *liked* the way the hotel looked after its guests.

4 I speak German *very well*.

5 *I'm OK about* working weekends.

6 *I'm free to* work in July and August.

7 Would you like me to *come for* an interview?

8 I have had *a lot of* experience of this kind of work.

> attend   considerable   enjoyable   fluently   receive
> to be available for   to be impressed by   to be willing to

6 Think about paragraphing

Look back at **Letter B** on p.17. Complete the outline of the letter in the table below.

Paragraph	Main topic	Details
1		
2		
3		
4		

7 Think about grammar

Relative clauses

a Look at the following sentences from **Letter B**. The **bold** word in each sentence is a relative pronoun. Which word or idea does it refer back to?

*I am writing to apply for the job of information officer, **which** was advertised in 'The Daily News'.*

*I worked as a guide last summer with Blue Sky Holidays, **which** I enjoyed very much.*

b Join the following pairs of sentences, using a relative clause for each one.

1 I went to the USA last summer. I improved my English a lot in the USA.

....

2 I worked with Mr Andrews. Mr Andrews taught me how to use a computer.

....

3 I am studying French. I enjoy studying French very much.

....

4 I enclose the names of two people. The two people can give you references for me.

....

5 I work in an office. There are many foreign visitors in the office.

....

Exam practice: Write a letter

You are going to write a letter on the topic below.
Do the tasks which follow.

You have just read the advertisement which appears opposite on the noticeboard in your school.

You have decided to apply for the scholarship. Write your **letter of application** (120–180 words).
Do not write any addresses.

- **Think about your reader**

  What is the correct greeting and ending for your letter?

- **Think about paragraphing**

  Use the following outline for your letter:

  1 State your reason for writing.

  2 State the scholarship you are applying for.

  3 Say where you saw the advertisement.

  4 In the main paragraphs of the letter, use a new paragraph each time you start to write about a new topic.

  5 In the last paragraph, say where you can be contacted.

- **Think about style**

  Remember to use formal vocabulary and expressions.

- **Edit your text**

  Check your writing for errors when you have finished.

> THIS YEAR, the school is offering a travel and study scholarship to all students who have studied at the school for three years or more. You will travel to Britain, and study English for three months in Oxford, all expenses paid.
>
> **Please apply in writing, saying why you deserve this scholarship, to Nicholas Simms within two weeks.**

Further practice

Write a letter on the topic below.

You have just read the advertisement opposite in a newspaper.

Write your **letter of application** (120–180 words).
Do not write any addresses.

> ### GROUP LEADERS REQUIRED
>
> Fit, enthusiastic people required to work with groups of foreign children (aged 11+) visiting this area in July and August.
> We are looking for people who:
> - like working with children
> - can speak at least two foreign languages
> - have previous experience of organising sports and other activities
>
> Apply in writing to Jim Aston, Adventure Holidays, PO Box 4598, explaining why you would be suitable for the job.

5 Making a request

1 Read the question

In Part 2 of the exam, you may be asked to write a formal letter in which you make a request. **Read the exam question below and underline the key words. Use the question which follows to help you.**

> You recently stayed in a small hotel while on holiday in Britain, where the service was excellent and Mr Wilson, the manager, made sure your stay was very enjoyable. Unfortunately, you left your glasses behind in the hotel. Write a letter to the manager, asking him to send your glasses back to you. Offer to pay for any expenses.

Write your **letter** to the hotel manager (120–180 words). Do not write any addresses.

Why are you writing the letter? Tick (✓) the reasons that apply to the question.

a to apologise   **c** to describe your holiday

b to ask for something   **d** to offer to pay for something

2 Think about your reader

Work with a partner. Look at the exam question again and answer the following questions.

1 Who is going to read your letter?

2 What is your relationship to the reader?

  a someone you know well

  b someone in your family

  c someone you have met, but don't know well

  d someone you have never met

3 What style of writing should you use?

  a very informal and chatty

  b very formal and polite

  c fairly formal and polite

4 Which of the following greetings and endings are suitable for your letter?

  a Dear Mr Wilson, … Best wishes, Katy

  b Dear George, … Love, Katy

  c Dear Mr Wilson, … Yours sincerely, Katy Elliot

  d Dear Mr Wilson, … Yours faithfully, Katy Elliot

3 Brainstorm the topic

Work with a partner. Imagine the situation in the exam question and answer the questions.

1 Where was the hotel?

2 Why was the service good? What did the manager do to make your stay enjoyable?

3 Where might you have left your glasses?

4 Who might have found them?

5 What do your glasses look like?

6 How could the hotel send them to you?

7 Who should pay the expenses of sending the glasses to you?

8 What else would you say in your letter?

> **tip**
>
> If the situation in the question is not one you have experienced personally, spend some time trying to imagine it. It helps to close your eyes!
> - Think of names for the people.
> - Think of the ways people behave in the situation.
> - Think how you would feel in the situation.

4 Read a model text

Read the model text. Has the writer used the correct greeting and ending for the letter?
Is the letter in a suitable style?

Dear Mr Wilson,

I am writing to thank you very much for making my stay so enjoyable. I really appreciated your advice on sightseeing and having fresh fruit in my room every day.

I wonder if I could also ask you a favour. I realised when I got home that I had left my glasses behind. They have gold frames, and are in a dark red plastic case, which has my name and address written on the inside. I think I must have left them in the restaurant during breakfast on the day I left.

If you manage to find my glasses, could you please post them to me, by registered mail, to my home address? Of course, I will pay for the postage. Would it be possible for you to let me know how much this is? I will send you a cheque as soon as I hear from you. I would be very grateful if you could do this for me.

Please contact me if you have any problems with this matter, and once again, I would like to thank you for all your help.

Yours sincerely,

Katy Elliot

Katy Elliot

5 Think about paragraphing

Read the model text again, and complete the outline of the letter in the table below.

Paragraph	Topic sentence	Details
1 Introduction		
2		
3		
4 Conclusion		

6 Think about topic sentences

a Match the following topic sentences to the correct set of details.

1 I'm writing to thank you for all your help while I was in England.

2 Unfortunately, I forgot to pack my address book.

3 Luckily, my sister is going to England next week.

a It's a small black book with my name on the cover. I think I left it in the cupboard beside the bed. Could you please look for it?

b I'm sure I would have got completely lost in the city without your map. I also want to thank you for making phone calls to help me find a good car rental company.

c Would it be possible for her to pick up the address book? She will phone you when she arrives to arrange a suitable time.

b Write three details for each of the following topic sentences.

   1 I would like to thank you for sending me the information about Scotland.

   2 I was in such a hurry when I left that I left my camera behind.

   3 My brother is coming to London on 15th August for a holiday.

c Write a suitable topic sentence for each of the following sets of details.

   1 I had a superb holiday, and you were very kind to arrange my transfer to the airport at the end of my stay.

   2 It's a blue fountain pen, with a silver top, and it was a present from my grandmother. I think I left it at reception, next to the telephone.

   3 She will be arriving on Friday 19th November. Would it be possible for her to come to the hotel and pick up the bag? I have given her your address and phone number.

7 Think about vocabulary

Rewrite the following sentences, thanking the person and using a noun instead of the adjective. Make any necessary changes.

e.g. You were very **kind** to help me with my problems.

*Thank you for your **kindness** in helping me with my problems.*

1 You were very generous to spend so much time with me.

   ....

2 You were very helpful when I needed to know something.

   ....

3 You were very hospitable during my stay in your hotel.

   ....

4 You were very patient with my terrible English!

   ....

5 You were very efficient to send me the brochure so quickly.

   ....

6 You were very encouraging when I tried to speak English.

   ....

7 You were very cooperative when I had to change my hotel booking.

   ....

8 You were very sympathetic when I received the bad news.

   ....

8 Think about language

Requesting

a Look at the following sentences from the model text on p.21. They are polite, formal ways of asking someone to do something. Underline the phrases which make a request. What verb forms are used?

   ... could you please post them to me, ...?

   Would it be possible for you to let me know how much this is?

   I would be very grateful if you could do this for me.

tip

Use *would/could* + infinitive to make your requests more polite.

b Rewrite the following requests in a more polite, formal way.

1 Please arrange for a taxi to meet me at the airport.

....

2 Can you give me a lift to the station?

....

3 Please tell me how much it will cost.

....

4 Can you look for my jacket?

....

5 Can you send me information about your school?

....

Exam practice: Write a letter

You are going to write a letter on the topic below. Do the tasks which follow.

> You recently travelled by plane from London to your country. The service was excellent, and the cabin staff very helpful. When you got home, you realised that you had left a book on the plane. Write a letter to the airline company, asking them to return your book to you. Offer to pay for any expenses.

Write your **letter** to the airline company (120–180 words). Do not write any addresses.

- **Read the question**

  Underline the key words in the question, and identify the reader.

- **Brainstorm the topic**

  Imagine yourself in the situation in the question to get ideas.

- **Think about paragraphing**

  Make an outline for your letter, with topic sentences for each paragraph, as follows:

  Paragraph 1 – Introduction, thanking

  Paragraph 2 – Describe the problem and the book

  Paragraph 3 – Ask for help

  Paragraph 4 – Conclusion

- **Think about style**

  Choose an appropriate style of writing for your letter. Make sure you use polite ways of requesting.

- **Edit your text**

  Check your writing for errors when you have finished.

Further practice

Write a letter on the topic below.

> You have recently written to a college in Britain, asking for brochures about language courses. The director, Mrs Davis, was very efficient, and you received your brochure very quickly. However, you forgot to ask for a price list and a course timetable. Write a letter to Mrs Davis, asking her to send you a price list and an up-to-date timetable.

Write your **letter** (120–180 words). Do not write any addresses.

6 A letter to the editor

1 Read the question

In Part 2 of the exam, you may be asked to write a formal letter giving your opinion on a topic, e.g. to the editor of a newspaper or magazine, or to the town council. **Read the exam question below and underline the key words. Use the questions which follow to help you.**

You have just read the following letter in the Letters Page of an English-language magazine:

> Dear Sir/Madam,
>
> Why doesn't the government ban cars from driving in the city centre? It's very noisy and polluted, and the number of cars on the road is growing every day. I believe that we should keep the city centre for people, not cars.
>
> Yours faithfully,
>
> J. Manners

Write a **letter** to the editor, saying whether you agree or disagree with the writer of this letter (120–180 words). Do not write any addresses.

1 What is the topic of the letter written by J. Manners?

2 What is J. Manner's opinion about this topic?

3 What should your letter include?

  a a description of the traffic problems in your city

  b a discussion of your own opinion of the ideas in the letter

  c a discussion about pollution in general

  d a balanced argument for and against the opinion in the letter

2 Think about your reader

Work with a partner. Look at the exam question again and answer the following questions.

1 Who is going to read your letter?

2 Which greeting and ending is suitable for your letter?

3 What style of writing should you use?

3 Think about vocabulary

a Write the words in the box in the correct category.

Vehicles: ....

Problems: ....

Fuel: ....

Places to drive/walk: ....

Parking: ....

Adjectives: ....

People: ....

> air pollution   asthma   bus   bypass   car park   coach   crossroads   crowded   cyclist   diesel
> driver   exhaust fumes   filthy   frustrating   junction   lorry   motorbike   motorway
> noise pollution   noisy   pavement   pedestrian   smelly   the rush hour   to park   traffic jam
> unleaded petrol   van

b Look at the adjectives in **a**. What nouns can these words describe? Complete the table.

Adjective	Can describe:
frustrating	
filthy	
smelly	
crowded	
noisy	

c Write a sentence for each adjective in **b** with a suitable noun.

e.g. frustrating/traffic jams

The worst thing about traffic jams is that they are so frustrating.

4 Brainstorm the topic

Work with a partner and answer the questions. Make notes of your main points.

1 Are cars allowed to drive in the centre of the town where you live? If they are, what problems does this cause?

2 What problems might this cause in the future?

3 Imagine that all cars are banned from driving in the city centre. What advantages and problems might there be? Use the following ideas to help you.

- getting to work
- making deliveries to shops
- pollution
- health
- parking
- safety

Add any other ideas to the above list.

5 Read a model text

Read the model text and answer the following questions.

1 Does the writer agree or disagree with the letter in the exam question on p.24?

2 What style of writing does the writer use?

Dear Sir/Madam,

I have just read a letter in your magazine about banning cars from the city centre. I am strongly in favour of this idea.

Firstly, we have a serious problem with air pollution in our city. If cars were banned, there would not be so much pollution, and people's health would improve. The trees and plants in our parks and streets would also flourish.

Furthermore, many people are already tired and frustrated when they arrive at work, because they get stuck in traffic jams in the rush hour every day. If there were no cars allowed in the city, people would use public transport more, and perhaps even walk to work.

Finally, parking in the city is so difficult that cars are parked on the pavements, and pedestrians have to walk in the road. Without cars in the centre, the pavements would be free for pedestrians to do their shopping safely.

I think the government should do something about this urgently. Do any more readers feel the same way?

Yours faithfully,

P. Kensit

P. Kensit

6 A letter to the editor

6 Think about paragraphing

a Look back at the model text on p.25. How many paragraphs are there in the letter?

b Complete the following ideas map of the model text. Write the main topic of each paragraph in the numbered spaces, and then add the details.

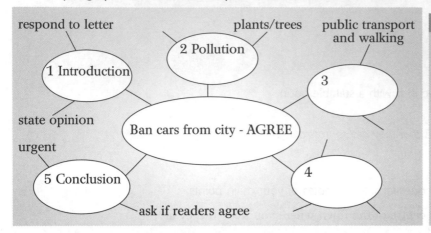

c Make an ideas map for another letter which disagrees with the letter in the exam question on p.24. Use your notes from **4 Brainstorm the topic** to help you.

7 Think about language

Expressing opinions

a Look at the sentences from the letters in this unit. Underline the phrases which show that the writer is giving an opinion.

I believe that we should keep the city centre for people, not cars.

I am strongly in favour of this idea.

I think the government should do something about this urgently.

b Write an expression which means the opposite of the following opinions. Sometimes more than one answer is possible.

1 I believe (that) ... *I do not believe (that) ...*

2 I agree (that) ... .

3 I am (strongly) in favour of ... .

4 It's disgusting/terrible/a shame that ... .

8 Think about your introduction

a Look back at the model text on p.25. In the introduction, the writer:

• says where he/she has seen the letter.

• says what the topic of the letter is.

• responds to the opinion expressed in the letter in the magazine.

b Read the following statements from different letters to the editor. Decide if you agree or disagree with the opinion, and write an introduction following the checklist in **a**.

1 It's disgusting that the town council does not have a recycling scheme for rubbish.

2 Have you seen the beaches recently? They are covered with rubbish and oil. In my opinion, the government must do something before we lose all our tourists.

3 I visited the local zoo recently, and was horrified to see animals in small, dirty cages. This zoo should be closed, and the animals returned to their natural habitat.

9 Think about grammar

Hypothetical situations

a Look back at the exam question on p.24. *Is* there a law banning cars from the city?

b To write good arguments, it is important to imagine what the city would be like if the government banned cars. Look at the following sentences from the model text on p.25, and underline the verbs. What form of the verb is used?

If cars were banned, there would not be so much pollution, …

The trees and plants in our parks and streets would also flourish.

If there were no cars allowed in the city, people would use public transport more, …

Without cars in the centre, the pavements would be free for pedestrians to do their shopping safely.

c Write answers to the following questions, using the second conditional to talk about a hypothetical situation. Write two or three arguments for each question.

1 What would the world be like without electricity?

2 What would your city be like if there were no police officers?

3 What would your school be like if there were only boys or only girls?

10 Think about connectors

a Look back at the model text on p.25. Underline the topic sentences for paragraphs 2, 3 and 4.

b The writer makes three main points. Look at each topic sentence and circle the word used to introduce each point.

c Look at the three topics you wrote about in **9 Think about grammar c**. Rewrite your sentences, linking your arguments with suitable connectors.

Useful expressions for sequencing ideas

When you introduce a number of ideas in order, use the following expressions:

The first idea	**The last idea**
Firstly, …	Finally, …
First of all, …	A final point is …
In the first place, …	Lastly, …

Following ideas
Furthermore, …
In addition,…
Another point is …

Exam practice: Write a letter

You are going to write a letter on the topic below. Do the tasks which follow.

You have just read the following letter in an English-language newspaper:

> Dear Sir/Madam,
>
> Today's teenagers have far too much freedom, and don't get any discipline from their parents. They're always out late at night, standing on street corners. I think that parents should be much stricter with their children. I'm sure that many other readers will agree with me.
>
> Yours faithfully,
>
> Mr H. Blackwell

Write a **letter** to the editor, saying whether you agree or disagree with the writer of this letter (120–180 words). Do not write any addresses.

- **Read the question**

  Underline the key words, identify your reader and the style you will use.

- **Think about paragraphing**

  Use an ideas map or a table to make an outline for your letter.

- **Think about language**

  Make sure you use suitable expressions for stating your opinion.

- **Think about grammar**

  Use the second conditional for discussing hypothetical situations.

- **Think about connectors**

  Don't forget to use connectors to introduce the topic sentences.

- **Edit your text**

  Check your writing for errors when you have finished.

Further practice

Write a letter on the topic below.

> You have just heard that the town council may build a new motorway in your area. The motorway would go through the middle of a large park, which would be destroyed.

Write a **letter** to the town council, opposing or supporting this plan (120–180 words). Do not write any addresses.

7 Asking for information

1 Read the question

a In Part 1 of the exam, there is only **one** question, which you **must** answer. This question asks you to write either a formal or an informal letter. Read the exam question below. What differences do you notice between this question, and the Part 2 questions in Units 1–6? **Underline the key points you must include in your letter**.

You have seen the following advertisement in a newspaper. Your family is interested in booking a holiday, but you would like more information.

Read the advertisement carefully and the notes which you have made for yourself. Then write to Paradise Beach Chalets, covering the points in your notes and adding any other relevant information.

Ideal for families!

Paradise Beach Chalets offer you self-catering holidays at incredible prices!

How many bedrooms?

Our small chalets have a double bedroom, with separate bathroom and kitchen, and large chalets sleep 4–6 people. Right beside the sea, with water sports available. Good shopping and interesting historical buildings in the nearest town.

Which ones?

How far?

- must be in early August, or early October
- price?
- childcare facilities?
- restaurant nearby?

Write a **letter** of between **120** and **180** words in an appropriate style. Do not write any addresses.

b In Part 1 questions, most of the information for your letter is given to you. Tick (✓) the key points you must include in your letter.

1 ask about facilities for children

2 ask about bedrooms in the large chalets

3 ask for information about historical buildings

4 ask which water sports are available

5 say you would like more information

6 give some information about how you will travel

7 ask the distance to the nearest town

8 say when you want to come

9 ask how much it costs

10 ask about television in the rooms

11 ask where the nearest restaurant is

12 ask where the nearest shops are

exam tip

To pass Part 1 of the exam, you must include all the necessary information given in the exam question. A letter written in very good English, but missing some information, will get a lower mark than one which has mistakes, but all the information.

2 Think about your reader

a Can you remember how to start and end letters? Complete the following greetings and endings for formal and informal letters. (See **Writing Bank**, p.124.)

Informal letters

When you write an informal letter, you begin and end:

.... Susan, … .... or ....,

Christopher

Formal letters

When you know the name of the person you are writing to, you begin and end:

.... Mr Smith, … ...., Christopher Williams

When you do not know the name of the person, you begin and end:

...., … ....,

Christopher Williams

b For the letter to Paradise Beach Chalets, which greeting and ending will you use? Should the letter be in a formal or informal style?

3 Think about vocabulary

a Write the words in the box in the correct category. (Some of the words can go in more than one category.)

Places to stay: ....

Hotel facilities: ....

Summer activities: ....

Winter activities: ....

> **beauty salon   bed and breakfast   buying souvenirs   campsite   caravan   diving   guest house**
> **gym   lift   room service   sailing   sauna   sightseeing   skating   skiing   snowboarding**
> **sunbathing   surfing   tennis court   top-class hotel**

b Check you know the meaning of the words *package holiday*, *vacancy* and *resort*.

4 Read a model text

a Read the model text. Has the writer included *all* the necessary information?

Dear Sir/Madam,

With reference to your advertisement in *The Times,* I am writing to ask for more information about Paradise Beach Chalets.

First of all, I would like to know if you have any vacancies in early August or early October. We are a family of four, and we would like to stay for two weeks. I would be grateful if you could tell me the price for two small chalets, and the price for one large one. As we have two small children, is there a babysitting service, if we want to go out in the evening?

Could you also give me some more information about the chalets? Could you tell me how many bedrooms the large chalets have? I would also like to know if there is a restaurant nearby and how far the nearest town is.

Finally, I would like to know what water sports are available, and how much they cost.

I look forward to hearing from you.

Yours faithfully,

Mr James Carrick

Mr James Carrick

---

7 Asking for information

b What other relevant information has the writer included in the letter, besides the information that must be included from the question?

c Read the model text again and complete the outline of the letter in the table below.

Paragraph	Main topic	Details
1 Introduction	*where advertisement seen* *reason for writing*	*The Times* *more information*
2 Main paragraph		
3 Main paragraph		
4 Main paragraph		
5 Conclusion	*ask for a reply*	*I look forward to hearing from you.*

5 Think about paragraphing

a Look at this list of information that must be included in a letter to a language school in Britain. Work with a partner and decide:

- which items belong in which paragraph.
- which order the items should be in each paragraph.

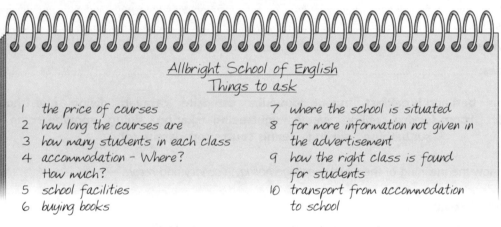

Allbright School of English
Things to ask

1   the price of courses
2   how long the courses are
3   how many students in each class
4   accommodation – Where? How much?
5   school facilities
6   buying books
7   where the school is situated
8   for more information not given in the advertisement
9   how the right class is found for students
10 transport from accommodation to school

b Make an outline for your letter.

6 Think about your introduction

a The introduction to transactional letters is usually very short. Look at the introduction to the model text on p.29 and underline the following phrases:

- where the writer says he saw the advertisement.
- the reason for writing.

With reference to your advertisement in 'The Times', I am writing to ask for more information about Paradise Beach Chalets.

exam tip

The questions in Part 1 do not usually say where the advertisement is from. You can use the name of a real newspaper, or an imaginary one. Common British newspapers are:

The Times	the *Sun*	the *Guardian*
the *Daily Mirror*	the *Independent*	the *Daily Express*
the *Daily Mail*	the *Daily Telegraph*	

Useful expressions for replying to advertisements

You can use the following expressions to begin any letter where you reply to an advertisement:

With reference to …

I am writing to …

b Write introductions to reply to the following advertisement.

1

Rent a furnished flat in Paris

Short stay specialist. Paris Appartements, 297 Avenue des Champs-Élysées, Paris

2

Short stay accommodation £79 per night

Sleeps 4. Quality and value. London Tourist Board inspected.

Robert and Polly Baker,
Short Stay Apartments,
73 Knaresborough Place,
Kensington, London SW5

7 Think about grammar

Indirect questions

a Look at the sentences (1–3) below from the model text on p.29. Each sentence contains a polite phrase to introduce an indirect question. Underline the indirect questions in the examples and then write each one as a direct question.

e.g. I would like to know *if you have a swimming pool.*

Do you have a swimming pool?

1 I would like to know if you have any vacancies in early August or early October.

....

2 I would be grateful if you could tell me the price for two small chalets, …

....

3 Could you tell me how many bedrooms the large chalets have?

....

b What differences do you notice about the verbs in the two types of question?

c Use the polite phrases in the box below, and write indirect questions from the set of notes.

Polite phrases

I would like to know …

Could you tell me …?

I'd be very grateful if you could …

Notes for letter to Majestic Hotel

1 swimming pool?
2 How much/double room?
3 vacancies/in June?
4 How far from airport?
5 organise sightseeing trips?
6 shops nearby?
7 Which bus/airport to hotel?
8 all rooms/have sea view?

7 **Asking for information**

Exam practice: Write a letter

You are going to write a letter on the topic below. Do the tasks which follow.

You have seen the following advertisement in a newspaper. Your family is interested in booking a holiday, but you would like more information.

Read the advertisement carefully and the notes which you have made for yourself. Then write to the White Mountain Ski Resort, covering the points in your notes and adding any other relevant information.

Action-packed holidays for the whole family!

classes for children?

Learn to ski at the White Mountain Ski Resort in the most beautiful part of Switzerland. Learn the basics with our instructors in just three lessons. Sm<u>all classes</u>. All rooms have a TV and open fire. Evening entertainment provided.   *How many people?*

What exactly?

- *must go in first two weeks of January*
- *need to bring own skis? Can we hire?*

- *instructors speak English?*
- *separate bathroom with the rooms?*

Write a **letter** of between **120** and **180** words in an appropriate style.
Do not write any addresses.

- **Read the question**

  Underline the key points in the question. Decide what details you should give about your family, besides the information you must include from the question.

- **Think about your reader**

  Choose the correct greeting and ending for your letter.

- **Think about your introduction**

  Choose an introduction for your letter. (See p.30.)

- **Think about paragraphing**

  Make an outline for your letter, with the points to be included in each paragraph.

- **Think about your conclusion**

  Choose a sentence to finish your letter. (See **Writing Bank**, p.125.)

- **Think about grammar**

  When asking for information, make sure you write mostly indirect questions. (See p.31.)

- **Edit your text**

  Check your writing for errors when you have finished.

Further practice

Write a letter on the topic below.

You are planning a holiday with a friend, who has sent you a letter with a hotel
advertisement. Read the letter and the advertisement carefully, and the notes which your
friend made. Then write to the hotel asking for the information which your friend
suggests, and adding any relevant questions of your own.

I saw this advertisement and thought it looked very good value for
money. I've made some notes about information I think we need. I'm
going away for a week, so could you write for more details? Can
you think of anything else we need to know?

Thanks. See you soon.

Oasis Hotel

Special offer – half price on all rooms
this summer!

still available in September?

Spend your holiday in our top-class hotel for just
half our normal price. We are right on the beach,
which is perfect for sailing and windsurfing, and you
can enjoy all our wonderful hotel facilities without
worrying about the price. Sightseeing excursions
arranged.

cost of boat hire?

What are they?

Where to?

We are famous for our friendly service and excellent
restaurant. Our rooms are comfortable and
air-conditioned.

view of the beach?

meals included in offer?

But hurry! This offer is limited. For more details
contact the Manager.

Write a **letter** of between **120** and **180** words in an appropriate style.
Do not write any addresses.

Transactional letters

8 Giving information

1 Read the question

Part 1 questions have a lot for you to read before you start to write.

Read the exam question below and find:

- the information about the situation
- the instructions on what you have to read
- the instructions on what you have to write
- the information given that you will need to summarise for your reader

You are a college student in London, and two English-speaking friends living in your country are coming to visit you next month. During their visit, they would like to visit the historic city of York, and spend a few days there. You are planning to go with them. You have the following information from a travel agent. Read it carefully. Then write a letter to your friends, giving them some information about the three different ways of travelling to York. Suggest which you think is the best way, and explain why.

London to York – 340 km
Car hire: £35 a day plus petrol and insurance

TRAIN

London dep.	York arr.
06.00	09.35
07.25	11.00
09.15	12.50

Return fare: £75 (Friday and Saturday), £60 (all other days)

30% discount with a student card

COACH

London dep.	York arr.
13.30	19.45
15.30	21.45
18.30	00.45

Return fare: £40 (Friday and Saturday), £30 (all other days)

30% discount with a student card

Write a **letter** of between **120** and **180** words in an appropriate style.
Do not write any addresses.

2 Think about your reader

Work with a partner. Look at the exam question again and answer the following questions.

1 Who is going to read your letter? Underline the words in the question which tell you who you are going to write to.

2 What style of writing should you use?

3 Brainstorm the topic

a Work with a partner and answer the questions.

1 About how long does the journey take by train and by coach? Is travelling by car likely to be slower or faster?

2 Which form of transport leaves London in the afternoons?

3 Which form of transport arrives in York after midnight?

4 Which is the cheapest way to travel?

    a train on a Friday

    b coach on a Tuesday

    c car

    d coach on a Saturday

    e train on a Thursday

exam tip

In the exam, you will write too many words if you explain all the details of the information you are given (times, days, dates, etc.). It is important to summarise the key information in a way that your reader will understand.

b Complete the following extract from a letter, giving a summary of the travel information in the question and comparing the different ways of travelling.

> The cheapest way to travel is (1) .... (way/days), leaving London in the (2) .... (time of day), but we will arrive in York in the (3) .... (time of day). If we take the train, we can leave London in the (4) .... (time of day), but this is (5) .... (cost). Hiring a car for a few days is (6) .... (cost), and also probably (7) .... (speed) than the train.

c Discuss the advantages and disadvantages of the three ways to travel in the exam question. Make notes in the table below.

	Advantages	Disadvantages
Car		
Train		
Coach		

d Which way do you prefer to travel? Give reasons.

8 Giving information

4 Read a model text

Read the paragraphs of the model letter and number them in the correct order.

a

Another option is to hire a car. It will cost £35 a day plus petrol and insurance, so it is quite expensive. If we go for three days, I think it will be more than I can afford!

b

Dear Mario and Christine,

c

First of all, we could go by coach. It's the cheapest way to travel, especially if we use our student cards to get a discount. The only problem is that the journey takes over six hours, and I know how you get sick on coaches!

d

Love, Carla

e

Thanks for your letter. I am really excited that you're coming to visit next month. I think we'll have a great time in York. I've managed to get some information about travelling there.

f

Write back and let me know what you have decided, so I can book the tickets. I can't wait to see you!

g

The final choice is the train. It only takes about three hours, and we can arrive before lunch. If we travel on Monday-Thursday, or Sunday, it'll cost £60, and we can also get a student discount of 30%. I would prefer the train because it is faster and more comfortable than the coach.

5 Think about paragraphing

a Look at the three main paragraphs in the model text which are about the different ways of travelling. Which expressions helped you to put these paragraphs in the correct order? Underline these expressions.

Useful expressions to begin topic sentences		
Topic sentences make your writing clear and easy for your reader to understand. The following expressions can be used to begin topic sentences when discussing alternatives:		
The first	way	
A second	option	
Another	choice	is ...
The last	possibility	
The final		

b Look at the following sets of alternatives. Write a topic sentence to introduce each one, using an introductory expression from the box on p.36.

1 You want to go to Corfu with some English friends next month.

Ways to get to Corfu
- ferry
- plane
- drive

2 Some English friends have asked you about the best time of the year to visit your city.

The best time of the year to visit your city
- end of August
- early December
- Easter

3 You and your friends are going to spend a holiday together in your country.

Places to stay
- a hotel
- rent a room
- campsite

c Choose one of the topics from **b** and add details to each of your topic sentences, explaining the advantages/disadvantages of each alternative. Write a suitable introduction and conclusion to your letter.

6 Think about vocabulary

All of the following sentences have vocabulary errors. Explain the errors and write the correct word. Make any other necessary changes.

e.g. *I had a lot of luggages with me.* (Wrong form of the word. *Luggage* is an uncountable noun.)

I think our trip will be funny. (Wrong word. *Funny* is something that makes you laugh. The correct word is *fun.*)

1 The travel to Scotland takes about 10 hours by coach.

2 I'm very exciting about our trip to Paris.

3 I've got all the informations about the hotel.

4 There is a big parking next to the hotel, so we can leave the car there.

5 All the hotels were full, so we had to stay in a camping.

6 Accommodations in the city are very expensive.

7 We didn't hire a car because of the big cost.

8 The hotel has all kinds of entertainments.

9 My most preferred way to travel is by plane.

10 I've done many trips to New York.

7 Think about tenses

Future possibilities

a Look at the following sentences from the model text on p.36. What tenses are used to talk about future possibilities?

If we go for three days, I think it will be more than I can afford!

If we travel on Monday–Thursday, or Sunday, it'll cost £60, …

b Imagine you are considering three different times for your friends to have a holiday in your country. Make notes on the advantages and disadvantages of the different times in the table.

Times	Advantages	Disadvantages
Last two weeks in August		*very crowded*
First two weeks in December	*good time for skiing*	
Two weeks at Easter	*interesting – traditional celebrations*	

c Use your notes from **b** to write sentences.

e.g. *It will be very crowded if you come in the last two weeks in August.* OR

If you come in the last two weeks in August, it will be very crowded.

Exam practice: Write a letter

You are going to write a letter on the topic below. Do the tasks which follow.

Two English friends of yours would like to spend a holiday in the Greek islands. You are going to meet them in Athens, and travel with them. As you have been there before, they have asked you to give them some information. You have the following information from a travel guide. Read it carefully. Then write a letter to your friends, giving them some information about the three islands. Suggest which you think is the best and explain why.

Patmos

Very beautiful, one of the smaller Greek islands

A few nightclubs in the main town, rest of the island very quiet

Visit: St. John's Monastery

Getting there: 10 hours from Athens by ferry

Aegina

Closest island to Athens for tourists

A few nightclubs, two open-air cinemas, many good restaurants in the main town

Tourist resort on the west coast

Visit: Very beautiful ancient temple

Getting there: Frequent ferries, hydrofoils. About 1 hour from Athens

Cephalonia

Largest of the Ionian islands. Booming tourist industry on south coast. Some of the best beaches in Greece

Visit: The picturesque fishing village of Fiskardo. Historical and Cultural Museum in the main town of Argostoli

Getting there: Fly from Athens (45 mins) or 4-hour bus trip, then 2-hour ferry trip

Write a **letter** of between **120** and **180** words in an appropriate style. Do not write any addresses.

- **Read the question**

  Underline the key points you must include in your letter.

- **Think about your reader**

  Decide on the style of writing you will use.

- **Brainstorm the topic**

  Look at the three options and make a list of the advantages and disadvantages of each. Decide which island you prefer, and why.

- **Think about paragraphing**

  Make an outline for your letter. Decide how many paragraphs there will be, and the main topic of each one. Write the topic sentences for your paragraph using an expression from p.36 to introduce each option. Add details to the main topics, using first conditional sentences where needed.

- **Edit your text**

  Check your writing for errors when you have finished.

Further practice

Write a letter on the topic below.

You are working in a travel agency in Bournemouth, on the south coast of England, for the summer. A friend from your country would like to study English at a language school for two months, and has asked you to send some information. You have made the following notes after telephoning three schools in the area. Read them carefully. Then write a letter to your friend, giving him/her the information about the three schools. Suggest which one you think is the best and explain why.

Southwest School of English
Price: £89 a week
Courses: general, business, and exam preparation
Small school, quiet area
Class size: up to 16 students
Computers, video

Bournemouth Academy
Price: £115 a week
Courses: summer intensive, general English
Biggest school in the area, central location
Class size: no more than 8 students
Computers, video, cafeteria, library

Whitecliff Study Centre
Price: £245 a week
Courses: general and business
Summer only, courses held at the local university
Class size: one-to-one, small groups (2-4)
Cafeteria, excursions to local places of interest

Write a **letter** of between **120** and **180** words in an appropriate style.
Do not write any addresses.

9 Giving and asking for information

1 Read the question

a Read the exam question below and write *G* next to the information you have to give, and write *A* next to the information you have to ask. **Underline the key points you must include in your letter.**

You would like to improve your English. You have just seen the following advertisement on the noticeboard of your school:

> ### Want to speak better? Write better?
> ### Brush up on your grammar?
>
> Native speaker of English offers private lessons.
> All ages and levels. Reasonable prices.
>
> Please write to: Ms Carol McBride, giving details of:
> - *yourself*
> - *how much English you already know*
> - *what you want to improve*
> - *why you want to improve*

Read the advertisement carefully and the following notes which you have made for yourself. Then write a letter to Ms McBride, giving details as requested and asking for the information covered in your notes.

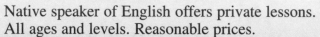

- price?
- time?
- place?
- class size?
- books provided?

Write a **letter** of between **120** and **180** words in an appropriate style.
Do not write any addresses.

b Look back at the advertisement in the exam question. What do you think *brush up on your grammar* means?

> **exam tip**
>
> Occasionally, the question may have one or two words you don't know. Don't panic! The questions are written so that the meaning of all the words is clear from the context. Make a guess at the word by looking at the whole situation described.

2 Think about your reader

Work with a partner. Look at the exam question again and answer the following questions.

1 Who is going to read your letter?
2 What style of writing should you use?
3 In the question, Ms McBride asks you for information about yourself. What personal information might she find useful?

3 Brainstorm the topic

Work with a partner and answer the questions.

How much you already know

1 How long have you been learning English?

2 Have you taken any exams in English?

3 Where have you studied English?

What you want to improve

1 What are the different aspects of learning English? Add to this list:

- grammar
- spelling
- listening

2 Look at the list you have just made. What are you good at?

3 What would you like to improve?

Why you want to improve

1 Why are you learning English? Which of the following reasons apply to you:

- English is an international language – it's useful for everybody.
- It will help me to get a job when I leave school.
- I want to pass the First Certificate, and other language exams.
- I want to go to an English-speaking country to study.
- I like the language and study for pleasure.

2 Can you think of any other reasons?

4 Compare two model texts

a Read the two letters and decide which you think would get a higher mark in the exam.

Letter A

Dear Ms McBride,

With reference to your advertisement for private lessons, I am writing to give you some details about myself, and to ask for more information.

I am 17 years old and a student at secondary school. It is very important for me to have a good level of English because I want to study English Literature at college.

I have been studying English for eight years at school. I think that I am good at grammar, but I have problems with vocabulary and I would like to improve this to help with reading and writing.

I would be very grateful if you could give me some more details about the lessons. Could you tell me how much you charge? Do you provide the books, or do I have to buy them? Also, I would like to know if the lessons are for one person, or for a group. Finally, could you tell me where and what time the lessons are?

The best way to get in touch with me is by phone, after 6.00 p.m. on 556 0908.

I look forward to hearing from you.

Yours sincerely,

Elena Maroniti

Elena Maroniti

Letter B

Dear Ms Carol,

I have seen your advertisement. I am a student and I want some lessons with you. I am not good at writing. Can you help me?

I am at school now, and I will finish in three years. Then I want to look for a good job in a hotel. I need good English to talk to all the tourists. My speaking is terrible, and if I don't improve I will not find a job. I want to know everything about your lessons, because you did not say everything in your advertisement. How much does it cost? Where do you give the lessons, at my house or yours? What time are the lessons? How many people do you have in a class? Do you give me a book or should I buy it?

That's all for now. Phone me (776 3452) in the evenings.

Best wishes,

George Zoulias

George Zoulias

b Read the two model texts on p.41 again and say why one is better than the other. Use the checklist to help you. Write *Yes* or *No* next to each question.

Writing checklist	Letter A	Letter B
1 Has the writer covered all the key points in the question?		
2 Does the letter have the correct greeting and ending for the reader?		
3 Is the letter written in the appropriate style?		
4 Is there an appropriate introduction?		
5 Does each main paragraph deal with a separate topic?		
6 Does each paragraph have a clear topic sentence where needed?		
7 When asking for information, does the writer use some indirect questions?		
8 Is there an appropriate conclusion?		

5 **Think about language**

Questions

a Look back at the exam question on p.40 and at the list of things you have to ask in your letter. Write as many questions as you can for each one.

e.g. price? *What is the price of each lesson? How much do you charge? How much per hour do the lessons cost?*, etc.

b Rewrite your direct questions from **a** as indirect questions. (If necessary, see p.31.)

exam tip

Put the information in the exam question into your own words as much as you can. If you copy directly from the question, you may lose marks. Remember to show the examiner your excellent knowledge of English!

6 **Edit your text**

Read the following letter, underline the errors and then correct them.

Dear Ms McBride,

I have seen your advertisement about English lessons. I would like to give to you some informations about myself, and ask to you some questions I have.

I am a 17 years old student at secondary school. I would like to improve my English because I am interesting to do a work in the tourist business.

I am learning English for three years in a private school. I am good in grammar, but I have difficulty to write very good. I would like to have lessons in writing essays.

I am grateful if you could tell to me some things about your lessons. I would like to know how much do they cost. Where are you giving the lessons? Could you tell me how many students do you have in your classes? Can I have lessons by my own?

Please give me a telephone (567 992).
I look forward to hear from you.

Yours sincerely,

Stephan Aris

Stephan Aris

Exam practice: Write a letter

You are going to write a letter on the topic below. Do the tasks which follow.

You recently entered a short story competition for students of English. You have just received this letter from the organisers of the competition, on which you have written some notes.

Congratulations! We are very pleased to inform you that your story has won first prize in our competition. You have won a three-day trip to London for you and a friend, and £200 to spend on books.

Your prize includes:

- free return flight —————— *transport from the airport?*
- accommodation for three nights ——— *Which hotel?*
- three meals a day——————— *must be taken at the hotel?*
- a sightseeing tour of London (optional) ——— *yes, please!*

We need to know what date you would prefer to travel, if you would like to go on the sightseeing tour, and any special arrangements you would like us to make for you. *yes!*

We look forward to hearing from you.

Yours sincerely,

Lindsey Green

Competition Organiser

Read the letter carefully. Then write a reply giving the information requested, and also covering the notes you have written on the letter.

Write a **letter** of between **120** and **180** words in an appropriate style. Do not write any addresses.

- **Read the question**

  Underline the key points you must include in your letter.

- **Brainstorm the question**

  Imagine you have just won this prize. How do you feel? What do you think is meant by *special arrangements*?

- **Think about paragraphing**

  Use the writing checklist on p.42 to plan your letter.

- **Edit your text**

  Check your writing for errors when you have finished.

Further practice

Write a letter on the topic below.

You saw an advertisement for a holiday cottage and contacted the owner for more details, making the notes you see opposite. You and two friends have decided to book the cottage for two weeks in the summer, and you would like to invite a fourth friend to join you.

Read the advertisement and the notes. Then write a letter to invite a friend of yours to join you, giving the necessary information and asking your friend for the information you need from him/her.

Summer holidays in Shakespeare country

Cottage within easy reach of Stratford. Visit Shakespeare Theatre, Shakespeare's birthplace, boat trips available on River Avon.
any interest to you?

Other attractions: hills nearby perfect for walking, sports centre 7 km away, swimming pool in Stratford (15 minutes on bus). Good public transport. Country cottage with 4 bedrooms, 2 bathrooms, modern kitchen. Beautiful garden with barbecue. Cleaner provided.

between four - price reasonable for you?

£175 per week, available only 29th June–15th July, or 12th–26th Sept.
Which dates suit you best?

Tel. 0554 39672 for more details

Write a **letter** of between **120** and **180** words in an appropriate style.
Do not write any addresses.

10 Making arrangements

1 Read the question

a Remember in Part 1 of the exam, there is only **one** question, which you **must** answer. **Read the exam question below and underline the key points you must include in your letter.**

Your English teacher has a British friend who is coming to visit your country. You have written to her, asking her to come and speak to your class about an aspect of life in Britain. You have received the following reply:

> I would be very happy to come to your school to speak to your class. I can come any time after 2nd April, but I am leaving for England on 10th April. Could you please write and tell me which day you would like me to come, and the time of the class? I would also like to know what subject your class would like to hear about. As I don't know your city very well, could you tell me about transport to the school? I'm staying at the Excelsior Hotel in the city centre.
>
> Yours sincerely,
>
> Stella Brown

Read Ms Brown's reply carefully and the set of notes which you have made for yourself. Then write a letter to Ms Brown, arranging the visit to your school. Make sure you answer all her questions, and cover all the points in your notes.

Stella Brown's visit
- *only two days possible: Friday 3rd, 8.00 p.m. or Saturday 4th, 11.00 a.m.*
- *subject of talk: 'How British teenagers spend their free time'*
- *bring photos for talk?*
- *transport: send a taxi to Excelsior Hotel*

Write a **letter** of between **120** and **180** words in an appropriate style. Do not write any addresses.

b In this letter, you have to give information and ask questions. Complete the notes in the table below.

I have to tell Ms Brown:	I have to ask Ms Brown:
Fri. 3rd or Sat. 4th only	Which day/prefer?

2 Think about your reader

Work with a partner. Look at the exam question again and answer the following questions.

1 Who is going to read your letter? What is Stella Brown's relationship to you?

2 What style of writing should you use?

3 What greeting and ending will you use for your letter?

3 Make a plan

a Look at the parts of the exam question you have underlined, and the notes in the table in **1 Read the question.** Put these points into the ideas map.

b Look at the topics you put in your ideas map. Decide which topics belong together in each paragraph. How many paragraphs will you have? Highlight the topics for each paragraph in a different colour.

c In which order will you write your paragraphs? Number the highlighted colours in order.

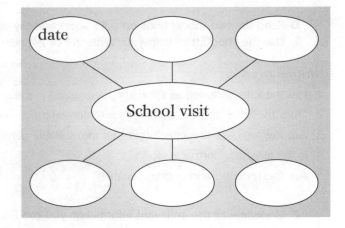

4 Compare two model texts

a Read the two letters and decide which you think would get a higher mark in the exam.

Letter A

Dear Stella,

Thanks a lot for agreeing to come and talk to our class. We're really looking forward to your visit! My phone number is 377 9963, so you can call me any time if you need my help. Maybe, I can tell you the best places to visit for sightseeing.

Now about the talk. I asked the class what they want to hear about and they told me that they want to know about how English kids spend their free time. I mean, what do they do for entertainment and sports? Do they eat out in restaurants, or do they go to cafés? If it's possible, bring photos of popular places for tourists to visit in your town. Don't worry about finding the school, because I will send a taxi to your hotel with careful directions about how to find the school.

If it's OK with you, we want the talk on Saturday morning at 11.00 a.m. Then we can have lunch in a great restaurant nearby, after you have finished the talk. I think about 20 people will come, and they are all about 15 years old. They like sports and going to the cinema.

You're very kind to do this for us. We're all crazy about the idea of speaking and listening to a British person. Not many foreigners visit our school, and we don't have any teachers from Britain here. If you don't like Saturday morning, we can have the talk on Friday night at 8.00 p.m.

Love,

Maria

Letter B

Dear Ms Brown,

Thank you very much for agreeing to come to our school to talk to our class. This will be a wonderful opportunity for the students in our school to listen and talk to a native speaker.

As most of our class are teenagers, we would like you to talk about 'How British teenagers spend their free time'. Would it be possible to bring some photographs to illustrate your talk? We are expecting an audience of about 20.

Can we have the talk on Saturday, 4th April, at 11.00 in the morning? Should this prove inconvenient for you, we could have it on Friday 3rd at 8.00 p.m. I would be grateful if you could tell me your preference. Because the school is rather difficult to find, I will send a taxi to your hotel to bring you to the school.

My phone number is 377 9963. If you need any help, or you would like me to meet you at the airport, please do not hesitate to call me. We are all looking forward to seeing you on the 3rd or 4th.

Yours sincerely,

Maria Fernández

Maria Fernández

10 Making arrangements

b Read the two model texts on p.45 again and say why one is better than the other. Use the checklist to help you. Write *Yes* or *No* next to each question.

Writing checklist	Letter A	Letter B
1 Has the letter included all the main points asked in the question?		
2 Does the letter contain any irrelevant information?		
3 Are the topics in the letter organised into suitable paragraphs?		
4 Is the language formal enough?		
5 Are the greeting and ending suitable?		

c Underline all the irrelevant information you can find in the letters.

d Underline all the examples of informal language you can find in the letters.

5 Think about your introduction

a Look back at the introduction to **Letter B** on p.45. Underline the phrase in which the writer thanks Stella Brown. What preposition and verb form follow *thank you*?

b In the introduction to **Letter B**, the writer thanks the reader for her help and then comments on how her help will benefit the students. Write introductions to the following letters in a similar way.

1 A letter to your pen friend, who has sent you posters of famous places in Britain to decorate your classroom and school.

2 A letter to a British publishing company, which has sent you a catalogue and some free copies of a student magazine.

3 A letter to an English friend of your teacher. You have sent her some money to buy and post a video to you of the English novel you are reading.

6 Think about your conclusion

a When you have made all the arrangements in the main paragraphs of your letter, your conclusion should:

- ask if the reader needs any more information.
- give a contact number or address.
- confirm the meeting place/date/time/first contact.
- say that you are looking forward to seeing/meeting the reader.

b Look at the expressions in the **Writing Bank** on p.125 and complete the following conclusion. (Sometimes more than one answer is possible.)

If you (1) .... any more information, please (2) .... me. My (3) .... is 377 9963. I (4) .... you at your hotel when you arrive to (5) .... our arrangements. We (6) .... all (7) .... to your visit.

c Write a conclusion for the following letters.

1 A letter to the head teacher of a group of students coming to spend a week at your school. You have arranged transport and evening activities. Confirm the arrangement to meet them at the airport at 6.45 p.m. on Friday 6th November.

2 A letter to the hotel manager, booking a room for an end-of-term party and presentation of certificates. Confirm the date, time, number of people, and the food and drink required. Arrange to go to the hotel on the 16th to pay.

7 Think about prepositions

Complete the following text with the correct preposition.
Use only one word in each space.

School trip – Final arrangements

To: All students

Thank you all (1) .... coming (2) .... the meeting last night. The final arrangements have now been decided. We will meet (3) .... the school (4) .... 9.00 a.m., (5) .... Thursday 12th June, where the bus will be waiting (6) .... us. Don't be late! You will need to bring your notebooks and pencils or pens, as well as a packed lunch, as we will go straight (7) .... the hotel. The trip should take (8) .... three hours. When we have checked (9) .... our rooms, we will meet (10) .... 4.30 p.m. (11) .... the hotel lobby (12) .... our first visit (13) .... a local pottery factory. I know that you have all been looking forward (14) .... this visit, and I hope you enjoy it!

Barbara Taylor, Head Teacher

---

8 Think about grammar

Gerunds and infinitives

a Look at the words in **bold** in the sentences from **Letter B** on p.45.

*Thank you very much for agreeing **to come** to our school.*

*… we would like you **to talk** about 'How British teenagers spend their free time'.*

*We are all looking forward to **seeing** you on the 3rd or 4th.*

---

tip
Some verbs are followed by a gerund, e.g. *agreeing*, and others are followed by an infinitive, e.g. *to agree*. When you note down vocabulary, also write if the words should be followed by a gerund or an infinitive. Writing an example sentence is useful to help you remember.

---

b Read this extract from a letter. Use the verb given in capitals at the end of each line and write the correct form of the verb in the space provided. Add the correct prepositions and make any other necessary changes.

I have finally decided what (1) ....   DO
George advised me (2) .... by bus,   GO
so I'm going to hire a car. I don't mind (3) ....,   DRIVE
and it will be a good opportunity for me (4) ....   STOP
and visit some places of interest on the way.
I'm considering (5) .... three days in Seville,   SPEND
and I have arranged (6) .... Sarah there.   MEET
This means that I will arrive on the 17th. Can you meet me
somewhere easy to find? I think I'm going to have difficulty
(7) .... your house without some help!   FIND
Instead (8) .... the first weekend at your house,   SPEND
why don't we go camping? Write and let me know what
you think. Once again, thanks very much (9) ....   INVITE
me. I'm really excited (10) ....   COME

    Love,
    Lucy

---

10 Making arrangements

Exam practice: Write a letter

You are going to write a letter on the topic below. Do the tasks which follow.

A group of English students is coming to your country for a week for an educational visit. You have been asked to be the guide for their visit. You have received the following letter from the head teacher of the school in Britain.

> Thank you for agreeing to be a guide for our group. I would like to know if you will meet us at the airport, and take us to our hotel. We would also like to know what sightseeing tours you have planned for us. We would prefer to go sightseeing in the mornings, and have our afternoons free.
>
> As this will be an educational visit, can you please make sure that you include places of historical or cultural interest? We would also like to have dinner at a restaurant which serves traditional local food on one of the evenings. Could you please write and confirm these arrangements?
>
> We are all looking forward to meeting you.
>
> Yours sincerely,
>
> *Helen Andrews*
> Head Teacher

Read the letter carefully and the notes which you have made for yourself. Then write a letter to Helen Andrews, making arrangements for the visit. Make sure you answer all her questions, and cover all the points in your notes. Add any other information you consider relevant.

- Meet at airport, taxis arranged to go to hotel
- Sightseeing: archaeological and cultural tours arranged by local tourist company
- Sightseeing from 10.30 a.m.-2.30 p.m., 4 days
- Restaurant – The Old Mill, with live folk music and dancing

Write a **letter** of between **120** and **180** words in an appropriate style.
Do not write any addresses.

- **Read the question**

  Read the question and underline the key points.

- **Think about your reader**

  Identify your reader and the appropriate style for your letter.

- **Think about paragraphing**

  Make an outline to organise the information into suitable paragraphs. Be careful to write only relevant information.

- **Think about your introduction and conclusion**

  Write an appropriate introduction and conclusion. (See **Writing Bank**, p.125.)

- **Edit your text**

  Check your writing for errors when you have finished.

Further practice

Write a letter on the topic below.

You have been asked to help organise your school's end-of-term party at a local hotel. Read the note from the organiser of the party, Pat, and the extract from the hotel's information leaflet. Then write to the hotel manager, making arrangements for the party, and giving information about your needs.

Could you write to Mr Masters, the hotel manager, and make the arrangements for the room, and the food and drink? Remember we want to present the students with their examination certificates, and give out prizes, so make sure there is a microphone in the room. These are the decisions we've made so far:

Date: 26th May
Time: 8–11.30 p.m.

Music: disco. Ask if the hotel can arrange this
Food and drink: enough for 60 people
Room: Ask if we can go in the day before and arrange tables, etc.

Thanks,

Pat

MAJESTIC HOTEL

for all your entertainment and business needs

We offer you the best facilities for weddings, christenings, parties, meetings and conferences. Choose from:

▼ **Executive Conference Hall – seats 120, stage, fully equipped with microphone, overhead projector, sound system**

▼ **Blue Room – dining area for 70 people, dancing area for when the party really gets going!**

▼ **Business Suite – small meeting rooms, seat 12–15 people. Conference table, telephone, fax. Computer connected to the Internet**

Please apply in writing to the Manager to book a room. Please note that for food and drink for parties of over 25, we require one week's notice.

Write a **letter** of between **120** and **180** words in an appropriate style.
Do not write any addresses.

11 Making a complaint

1 Read the question

Remember that in Part 1 of the exam there is only **one** question, which you **must** answer. **Read the exam question below and underline the key points you must include in your letter.**

You went on a weekend holiday with Cityworld Tours. Unfortunately, you were very disappointed in the holiday and did not enjoy it.

Read the Cityworld Tours advertisement carefully and the notes which you have made for yourself. Then, using the information, write a letter to Cityworld Tours, complaining about the holiday and asking for some money back.

Cityworld Tours

See the most interesting cities of Britain with our package weekend breaks. Included in the price:

- **all transport arranged**
- **comfortable rooms in top-class hotels near the city centre**
- **sightseeing tour with tourist guide in every location**

Book now!
You won't be disappointed!

Transport
- no transport arranged to get to hotel from station

Hotel
- lifts out of order
- hotel near construction site - very noisy

Sightseeing tour
- tourist guide clearly ignorant about the area

Write a **letter** of between **120** and **180** words in an appropriate style. Do not write any addresses.

2 Think about your reader

a Work with a partner. Look at the exam question again and answer the following questions.

1 Who is going to read your letter? What is the correct greeting and ending for the letter?

2 What style of writing should you use?

b Read the following extracts from letters of complaint, and decide which one would be successful in getting a refund. Which one is:

- not strong enough?
- too strong?
- appropriate in tone?

1
Your company should not be allowed to operate. You told lies in your advertisement, and I think the public should know about this. If you don't give me my money back, I will have to take you to court.

3
I was unhappy with the holiday, and I would be very grateful if you could please refund some of my money. If this is not possible, could you please offer me another holiday for free?

2
I believe you can appreciate how disappointed I was when the holiday turned out to be very different from the one advertised. I would like all or part of my money refunded.

> **tip**
>
> When you write a letter of complaint, it is important to get the tone of the letter correct. Try to be polite, state the facts clearly without showing too much feeling, and do not be too aggressive. Ask directly and politely for what you want.

3 Brainstorm the topic

Work with a partner and answer the questions.

1 If you pay money for something and are not happy with what you get, how do you feel?

2 Have you ever been disappointed with something you paid for? What happened? What did you do about it?

3 Imagine you are in the situation described in the question. How did you feel:

- before the holiday?
- when you checked in at the hotel?
- when you arrived at the station?
- on the excursion?

4 Read a model text

Read the following model text and decide if the following are appropriate:

- the greeting and ending
- the style of the letter
- the tone

Dear Sir/Madam,

I am writing in connection with your weekend breaks, which I saw advertised in *The Sunday Times*. I went on one of these breaks last week, and I am sorry to say that I was very disappointed.

Even though your advertisement stated that all transport would be provided, I had to take a taxi to the hotel. To make matters worse, the hotel refused to refund my taxi fare.

Furthermore, your advertisement promised a stay in a top-class hotel. However, the lift was not working at any time during the weekend, despite my repeated requests to have it repaired. In addition, the hotel was near a construction site and the constant noise was very irritating.

I also went on the sightseeing tour, which I had been looking forward to. I was very disappointed to find that the guide clearly knew nothing about the area.

I would like to hear your explanation for the above problems, and I would also like to have all or part of my money refunded.

I look forward to hearing from you.

Yours faithfully,

Claire Dawson

Claire Dawson

11 Making a complaint

5 Link your text

a Look at the following sentences from the model text on p.51. Underline all the linking words and phrases.

Even though your advertisement stated that all transport would be provided, I had to take a taxi to the hotel.

To make matters worse, the hotel refused to refund my taxi fare.

Furthermore, your advertisement promised a stay in a top-class hotel.

However, the lift was not working at any time during the weekend, despite my repeated requests to have it repaired.

In addition, the hotel was near a construction site and the constant noise was very irritating.

b Which of the words and phrases in **a** are used to:

- introduce a contrasting idea
- give more information

c Look at the advertisement below and the handwritten notes. Write a short paragraph for each complaint, using suitable linking words and phrases.

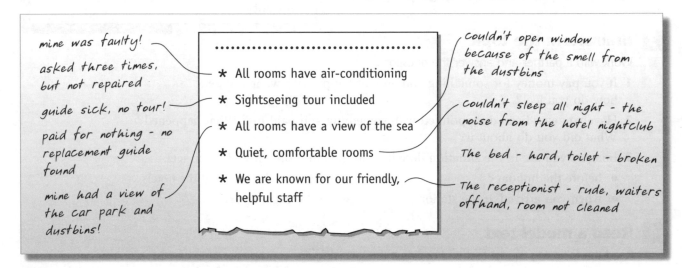

6 Think about paragraphing

Write the missing paragraphs of the following letter, using your sentences from **5 Link your text c**. Put the sentences and paragraphs into a suitable order.

Dear Sir/Madam,

I am writing in connection with the weekend I recently spent at your hotel. I have to say that I was very disappointed.

I am sure you will understand that I was very dissatisfied, and did not enjoy my weekend at all. I would like a full refund as soon as possible.

Yours faithfully,

John Waters

John Waters

7 Think about your introduction

a Look back at the introduction to the model text on p.51 and at the introduction in **6 Think about paragraphing**. What information does each writer include?

b Look at the **Writing Bank** on p.126 for ways to introduce a complaint, and write an introduction to the following letter.

> Your advertisement stated that the cost of all the meals would be included in the price. When I got the bill, I was appalled to find that I had to pay for them. Furthermore, the meals were cold, and the service in the restaurant was very slow.
>
> Your advertisement also promised that there would be a babysitter available in the hotel. When my husband and I wanted to go out for the evening, we were told that the babysitter was on holiday. The receptionist was very rude when I asked her to find someone else to look after my little girl.

8 Think about your conclusion

a Look back at the conclusion to the model text on p.51 and at the conclusion in **6 Think about paragraphing**. What does each writer say?

b Look at the **Writing Bank** on p.126 for ways to finish a letter of complaint. Write a suitable conclusion to the letter in **7 Think about your introduction**.

9 Think about vocabulary

Adjectives describing feelings

a Complete the following sentences, using the words and expressions in the box.

Mild feeling	Quite strong feeling	Very strong feeling
fed up	annoyed	appalled
inconvenienced	disappointed	disgusted
put out	dissatisfied	furious
taken aback	irritated	horrified

1 When something is not satisfactory, you feel ....

2 When you expect something good, and it turns out bad, you feel

....

3 When something makes you feel *extremely* upset, you feel

.... or .... or ....

4 When you feel *quite* angry, you are .... or

....

5 When something causes trouble or difficulty for you, you are

.... by it.

6 When you are *very, very* angry, you are ....

7 When something negative happens, and you are surprised by it, you are

.... by it.

8 When something upsets you *a little*, you are .... by it.

9 When you have had enough of a situation, you feel ....
with it.

b Some of the adjectives in **a** end in *-ed* and are passive in meaning. Some of these adjectives can have an *-ing* ending and are active in meaning.

e.g. *I was **disgusted** by the food.*

*The food was **disgusting**.*

Read the following extract from a letter about a disastrous holiday. Complete the extract using an appropriate word from **a** in the correct form. Use a different word for each answer.

In general, the holiday was (1) .... For a start, the food was (2) ...., and the service was slow. What's more, the telephone was ringing all night, which was very (3) .... Not only that, but I had to ask five times for my room to be cleaned; I was quite (4) ...., I can tell you. When I finally saw the bill, I was (5) ....! For that kind of money, I had expected a better hotel. It was all very (6) ....

10 Think about grammar

Reported speech

a In the exam question on p.50, the advertisement promised:

- all transport arranged
- top-class hotels
- all hotels near the city centre
- sightseeing tour with tourist guide in every location

These promises are in note form. Write a full sentence for each one.

e.g. all transport arranged   *All transport will be arranged.*

b In the model text on p.51, the writer reports what was promised and complains about what really happened. Look at this sentence from the model text, and the sentences you wrote in **a**. What form of the verb is used? Why?

Even though your advertisement stated that all transport would be provided, ...

c Imagine you went on one of the excursions in the advertisement opposite and you were very disappointed with your trip. Report what the advertisement promised, and add a complaint to each point.

Breakaway Excursions

▶ ▶ ▶ ▶ ▶ ▶ ▶ ▶ ▶ ▶ ▶ ▶

See the sights of the city with us!

Tours leave at 8.30 a.m. every day.

All our guides speak good English, French and Italian.

Our guides are very knowledgeable.

All tours include the price of lunch in a traditional restaurant.

Exam practice: Write a letter

You are going to write a letter on the topic below. Do the tasks which follow.

You bought the personal stereo advertised opposite from a mail order catalogue. Unfortunately, when you received it, you were very disappointed.

Read the advertisement carefully and the notes which you have made. Then, write a letter to Home Mail Order, complaining about the stereo, and asking for your money back, or a new stereo.

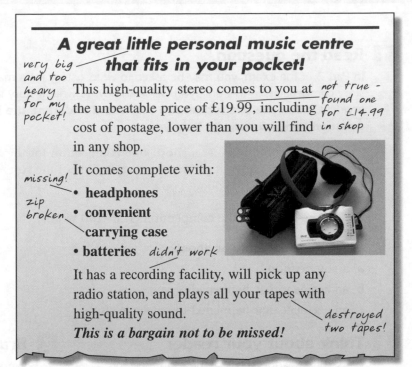

very big and too heavy for my pocket!

A great little personal music centre that fits in your pocket!

This high-quality stereo comes to you at the unbeatable price of £19.99, including cost of postage, lower than you will find in any shop.

not true – found one for £14.99 in shop

It comes complete with:

missing!

- **headphones**

zip broken

- **convenient carrying case**

- **batteries** *didn't work*

It has a recording facility, will pick up any radio station, and plays all your tapes with high-quality sound.

destroyed two tapes!

This is a bargain not to be missed!

Write a **letter** of between **120** and **180** words in an appropriate style. Do not write any addresses.

- **Read the question**

  Read the question and underline all the key points. Decide what style you should use.

- **Think about your introduction**

  Plan your introduction, with a reference to the stereo, and how you felt when you received it.

- **Think about paragraphing**

  Plan your main paragraphs. Write a topic sentence for each one, and add notes for the details.

- **Think about grammar**

  Use reported speech to talk about what the advertisement promised.

- **Think about your conclusion**

  Write your conclusion, stating what you want the company to do, and ask for a refund, or a new stereo.

- **Edit your text**

  Check your writing for errors when you have finished.

Further practice

Write a letter on the topic below.

You saw an advertisement for TV repairs, and took your TV to be mended. Unfortunately, you were very disappointed in the service they gave.

Read the advertisement carefully and the notes which you have made. Then write to the manager, complaining about the service you have received and asking for your money back.

Do you need a fast and reliable repair service?
Come to Express Service for all your TV, video and stereo repairs.

....
- ★ **fast service – all repairs ready in three days**
- ★ **very low prices**
- ★ **professional, careful repairs**
- ★ **friendly, helpful staff**

- *repair took 2 weeks*
- *TV still not working properly*
- *staff rude and unhelpful*
- *had to wait in shop 30 minutes, because only one assistant*
- *price was very high, more than another shop I visited*

Write a **letter** of between **120** and **180** words in an appropriate style. Do not write any addresses.

12 Describing an accident

1 Read the question

In Part 2 of the exam, you may be asked to write a story for a magazine, or for a short story competition. In this unit, you will learn how to write a story in which you describe an accident. **Read the exam question below and underline the key words. Use the question which follows to help you.**

> You have decided to enter a short story competition for the best story about an accident. The competition rules say that the title of the story must be *My worst day* and the story must be about you.

Write your **story** for the competition (120–180 words).

What must your story be about?

a a competition

b an accident that happened to you

c an accident that happened to someone else

2 Think about your reader

Work with a partner. Look at the exam question again and answer the following questions.

1 Who is going to read your story?

  a the judges of a competition

  b your friend

  c your teacher

2 What style of writing should you use?

  a formal and factual

  b personal and vivid

3 Brainstorm the topic

Work with a partner and answer the questions.

1 What kind of events could be considered accidents? Think about accidents that you have experienced, or have heard about from someone else, and make a list.

2 What sort of situations are suitable for writing about accidents? Add more possibilities to the following list.

- a school trip
- a sporting event
- something that went wrong at home
- something that went wrong at school or work

4 Read a model text

a Look at the following pictures, which show scenes of a story. Number the pictures in a suitable order and then tell the story to your partner.

b Read the following story, and compare it with the story you have just told. How is it different?

Have you ever done something very simple which turned into a disaster? Something just like this happened to me.

It was a bitterly cold winter's day. I had just moved into a new flat and most of my possessions were still in boxes on the lounge floor. While I was busy arranging the place exactly as I wanted, I began to feel chilly and switched on the central heating.

After about an hour, I noticed that all the heaters were stone cold. As I was fiddling angrily with the knobs on the top of the lounge radiator, a fountain of brown smelly water gushed from the pipes, soaking me to the skin. 'Oh no!' I gasped, as the water flooded the entire living room floor. I managed to turn the knob, and thankfully, the water stopped.

I spent the rest of the day and half of the night mopping up water, which had unfortunately soaked most of the boxes on the floor, and the things inside them.

I suppose that I learnt one thing – leave plumbing to the experts!

c Match the pictures in **a** to the different parts of the story.

d Read the model text again. Complete the outline of the story in the table below.

Paragraph + main topic	Details
1 Introduction	
2 Situation before the accident	
3 How the accident happened	
4 How the story ended	
5 Conclusion	

e Make an outline for an accident story of your own, following the example in **d**. Remember, *you* are the main character.

5 Think about your introduction

a Read the introduction to the model text again. How does the writer make you want to read on?

b A good introduction to a story usually gives the reader just a little surprising information with no details. This makes you want to read on, to find out what happened. Read the following sentences from introductions to stories about accidents, and decide which ones make you want to read on.

1 I slipped and twisted my ankle on a mountain walk one day last summer.

2 The day seemed perfectly normal until I got to the station.

3 Although I had often changed a flat tyre before, on this day things were a little different.

4 I was on my way to catch the ferry when my car broke down and I nearly missed the boat.

5 Have you ever tried to catch a runaway dog, and ended up in the police station?

6 The worst day I ever had was when I was on my way to take an important English exam, and the taxi I was in had an accident with a bus.

12 Describing an accident

c Choose one interesting introduction from **b** on p.57, and make notes of your ideas for the rest of the story.

d Look at the outline you made for your own story in **4 Read a model text e**. Write an introduction for it. Look at two more outlines from the students in your class. Write two more introductions.

6 Think about vocabulary

a When you are describing something, try to choose vocabulary that is vivid. Look at the following phrases, which are simple, vague ways to describe something. Find the words and phrases in the model text on p.57 which mean the same as the following, but which give a more vivid picture.

1 cold (three expressions)

2 turning

3 a lot of water

4 came out

5 making me wet

6 said

b Work with a partner and write more vivid words or phrases for the words in *italics* in the following sentences. Use your dictionary to help you.

1 It was a *nice* day for once, so we decided to go for a walk.

2 As I was swimming in the stream, the *cold* water felt *good*.

3 With his foot in plaster, he *walked* to the car.

4 I didn't like the way he was *looking* at me.

5 'Leave me alone, or I'll call the police!' I *said*.

6 The sun was *very hot* that day, and we soon got sunburnt.

7 As I turned the corner, I *saw* a group of people in the distance.

8 He was late. As soon as he got to the port, he *got* out of the car and *ran* towards the departing ferry.

7 Think about tenses

Narrative tenses

a Look back at the model text on p.57. Find all the verbs and decide which time they refer to (past, present or future).

b Look at the following examples from the model text. Underline the main verbs in each example.

While I was busy arranging the place ..., I began to feel chilly ...

I managed to turn the knob, and thankfully, the water stopped.

I spent the rest of the day and half of the night mopping up water, which had unfortunately soaked most of the boxes on the floor ...

Narrative tenses

- The Past Simple is used to express actions which follow each other in a story.
  I managed to turn the knob, and thankfully, the water stopped.

- The Past Continuous is used to express an interrupted past action.
  While I was busy arranging the place ..., I began to feel chilly ...

- The Past Perfect is used to express an action that happened before another action in the past.
  I spent the rest of the day and half of the night mopping up water, which had unfortunately soaked most of the boxes on the floor ...

C Use the notes below to write a story about an accident which happens while out walking on a mountain. Make complex sentences, using the Past Simple, Past Continuous and Past Perfect where appropriate.

- walk/mountain trail/sounds of birds/trees
- in forest/notice/sun/disappear/black cloud
- climb/steep part/mountain/I/slip/twist/ankle
- lie/ground/shout for help
- nearly/give up/hear/voices/distance
- shout/group of hikers/come/find me
- call/mountain rescue/come with stretcher
- put stretcher/ambulance/drop me!

Exam practice: Write a story

You are going to write a story on the topic below. Do the tasks which follow.

An English-language magazine for students is holding a competition for the best story about an accident that happened to you. The winning story will be published in the magazine. You decide to enter the competition. The story must have the title: *The day I'll never forget*.

Write your **story** for the competition (120–180 words).

- **Read the question**

  Read the question and underline the key words.

- **Think about your reader**

  Think about who will read your story and what vocabulary you can use. Write your story as if you were going to win!

- **Think about paragraphing**

  Make an outline for your story. For each paragraph decide on the main topic, and then add details.

- **Think about your introduction**

  Plan a good introduction which will make your reader curious.

- **Think about tenses**

  Check the tenses in your story.

- **Edit your text**

  Check your writing for errors when you have finished.

Further practice

Write a story on the topic below.

Your teacher is going to make a class magazine of your favourite stories. The stories must all include an accident with a funny side to it. Your teacher has asked you to write a story for the magazine.

Write your **story** (120–180 words).

13 Describing an event

1 Read the question

In Part 2 of the exam, you may be asked to write a description of an event you have attended, such as a wedding, a party, or another celebration of some kind. **Read the exam question below and underline the key words. Use the questions which follow to help you.**

Here is part of a letter written to you by your British pen friend:

> ... Anyway, they finally left on their honeymoon. We all thought it was a great wedding! Have you ever been to a wedding? What happened on the day? Who came to the wedding? Write and tell me all about it.

Write a letter to your pen friend, describing a wedding you have attended. Describe the events of the day and the people who came.

Write your **letter** (120–180 words). Do not write any addresses.

1 When you describe the wedding, what are the two points the question asks you to include?

2 What should you write?

  a a general description of a typical wedding in your country

  b a description of one wedding you have been to

3 What tenses should you use in your description?

2 Think about your reader

Work with a partner. Look at the exam question again and answer the following questions.

1 Who is going to read your letter?

2 What style of writing should you use?

3 Think about vocabulary

a Who might you see at a wedding? Work with a partner and make a list of words.

  e.g. *bride*

b Complete the following description of a church wedding in Britain, using the expressions in the box. Make any necessary changes.

When everyone is in the church, the bride arrives and
(1) .... towards the priest and her
husband-to-be. The bride's father (2) ....,
and the priest then (3) ....
When the rings have (4) ....,
the priest (5) .... the
couple. Then they (6) ....,
and leave the church. Outside, all the guests (7) ....
at the newly-weds. Then, (8) they ....,
and everyone goes to where the (9) .... Finally, the
happy couple (10) ....

bless the couple
exchange rings
give away the bride
have photographs taken
hold the reception
leave for their honeymoon
perform the ceremony
sign the register
throw confetti
walk up the aisle

C Who, at a wedding, might be described as:

1 nervous?   **4** beaming with pride?

2 tearful?   **5** moved by the ceremony?

3 fidgety?   **6** radiant?

4 Brainstorm the topic

Work with a partner and answer the questions.

1 Have you ever been to a wedding? Whose wedding was it? Who went to the wedding? Did you enjoy it?

2 Where did the wedding take place?

3 Can you describe what happened during the ceremony?

4 What did you do after the ceremony?

5 Did the married couple go on honeymoon? Where did they go?

exam tip

If the exam question asks you to write about an event you have never seen or been to, try to think about what you know of the event from TV programmes, what you have read, or from what other people have told you.

5 Compare two model texts

a Read **Letter A** below and **Letter B** on p.62 and decide which you think would get a higher mark in the exam.

Letter A

Dear Susie,

Thanks a lot for your letter. I really enjoyed reading about the wedding you went to.

My cousin got married last June. There were about 75 guests, wearing their best clothes, gathered in a little church in my family's village. The groom, who was pacing up and down inside the church, looked nervous, and my aunt looked decidedly tearful.

After 20 minutes, there was no sign of the bride. The priest, who was fidgeting nervously with his book, was obviously concerned. We all began to get more than a little anxious. When I next glanced at the groom, I saw a huge smile of relief on his face. As I turned, I saw my cousin, slightly flushed, but radiant as every bride should be, walking up the aisle. As they passed us, her father, who was giving her away, whispered, 'Ran out of petrol. Would you believe it?'

We had a great time after that, because the reception was held in a beautiful restaurant by a lake, which was a perfect end to the day.

Write back soon!

Love,

Natasha

Letter B

Dear Susie,

Thanks for your letter. I really liked reading about your sister's wedding.

In my country, all the family and friends of the couple go to the church. The bride and groom stand at the front near the priest, and everybody else stands behind. There is a best man, who stands behind the couple.

First of all, everybody waits outside the church for the bride to arrive. She usually comes with her father. Then everybody goes into the church, and the priest performs the ceremony. The priest speaks to the couple, and then they exchange rings. They then walk around the priest three times, while everybody throws rice at them.

After the church ceremony, everybody goes to a reception. It's a great day for everyone. Maybe you can come to a wedding with me when you visit us next year.

Write soon and tell me all your news.

Love,

Natasha

b Read the letters in **a** again and answer the following questions.

   1 Which letter is a description? Which one is a narrative?

   2 Which letter has answered the exam question correctly?

   3 Which letter uses good descriptive vocabulary?

   4 Which letter has rather simple sentence structure?

c Look back at **Letter A** on p.61. What is the topic of each main paragraph? Complete the following diagram.

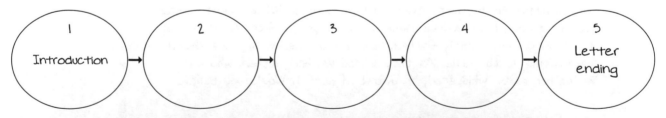

1 Introduction → 2 → 3 → 4 → 5 Letter ending

exam tip

- If you write an answer with no mistakes, but do not answer the question correctly, or fully, you will *not* pass.
- You will pass the question if you answer it fully, even if you have made some mistakes – as long as you do not make too many.

6 Think about grammar

Non-defining relative clauses

a Look at the following sentences from **Letter A**. The words in **bold** are in clauses which give extra information about the previous noun.

*The groom, **who** was pacing up and down inside the church, looked nervous, ...*

*The priest, **who** was fidgeting nervously with his book, was obviously concerned.*

Draw a line from the word in **bold** to the noun that it describes. What is the main verb in each sentence? Underline it.

b Join the following pairs of sentences, making one into a clause which gives extra information.

1 The children were running around the church. They were excited.

....

2 The bride's mother was dabbing her eyes with a tissue. She was looking upset.

....

3 The best man was talking to the groom. He was wearing a rose in his jacket.

....

4 The church was looking beautiful. It was decorated with flowers.

....

c Rewrite the following short extract to improve the style of writing. Join the sentences, using non-defining relative clauses where suitable and other appropriate methods of linking.

The bride was looking absolutely radiant. She was wearing a white silk dress. She was carrying a huge bouquet of white roses. Two small children were walking behind her. They were about five years old. They looked very sweet. They were wearing frilly, white dresses. They were carrying the train of the bride's dress. The bride's father was walking beside the bride. He was holding her arm. He was looking very proud. He turned to the guests and beamed.

Exam practice: Write a description

You are going to write a description on the topic below. Do the tasks which follow.

> Your English pen friend is doing a project on 'Festivals in other countries'. He/She has asked you to describe an interesting festival that you have been to recently in your country. Write a letter to your pen friend, describing what kind of festival it was, and what happened during the event.

Write your **letter** (120–180 words).
Do not write any addresses.

- **Read the question**

  Read the question and underline the key words.

- **Think about your reader**

  Identify your reader and the appropriate style for your letter.

- **Think about paragraphing**

  Make an outline for your letter as follows:

  1 In the introduction, thank your friend for his/her letter, and briefly give your recent news.

  2 In the second and third paragraphs, make notes about the topics asked for in the question.

  3 Write a topic sentence for each main paragraph.

  4 In the conclusion, ask for a reply, and send greetings.

- **Edit your text**

  Check your writing for errors when you have finished.

Further practice

Write a story on the topic below.

> You have decided to enter a short story competition organised by an English magazine that you read. The rules of the competition say that the story must have the title: *The best party I have ever been to.*

Write your **story** (120–180 words).

Stories

14 A journey

1 Read the question

In Part 2 of the exam, you may be asked to write a story about a journey.
Read the exam question below and underline the key words.

> A magazine is offering a prize for the best short story with the title: *A journey in bad weather.* You decide to enter the competition.

Write your **story** for the competition (120–180 words).

2 Think about your reader

Work with a partner. Look at the exam question again and answer the following
questions. (Sometimes more than one answer is possible.)

1 Who is going to read your story?

2 If you were the judge of the stories entered
for the competition, what qualities would
the winning story have?

  a a good introduction, giving the reader
    background information

  b a detailed description of the bad weather

c detailed descriptions of the people in the story

d a description of the events after the bad weather
  happened

e a good conclusion, with your thoughts about
  the experience

f a long description of where you were going
  and why

3 Brainstorm the topic

Work with a partner and answer the questions.

1 What means of transport can you use to
make a journey?

2 What different reasons can you think of for
making a journey?

3 What different places have you travelled to?

4 What was the weather like on these trips? Describe
bad weather you have experienced on a journey.

5 How did the bad weather affect you? How did it
affect other people on the journey? Did the
weather affect the journey in any other way?

6 How did you feel at the end of the journey?

4 Think about vocabulary

Write the words and expressions in the box in the correct category. Use the following headings.

Weather conditions **Adjectives** **Effects of bad weather**

> blizzard chilly choppy sea communications cut off delays downpour
> flooded streets fog freezing gale-force winds heat wave hold-ups humid
> icy conditions people get heatstroke people get seasick people get stranded
> poor visibility roads blocked by fallen trees ships pitch and roll slippery roads
> snowstorm stifling sweltering thunder and lightning traffic grinds to a halt
> treacherous conditions vehicles skid

5 Read a model text

a Read the model text on p.65 and identify what the writer is trying to say about the
journey. Choose from the sentences below.

1 Because of the bad weather, we had to cancel our trip.

2 In spite of the bad weather, we managed to reach our destination without a problem.

3 Due to the bad weather, we had many problems and were too upset to enjoy
the rest of the trip.

4 Although the weather was bad, we enjoyed our trip after all.

A few years ago, my family and I decided to have a holiday touring Ireland. We boarded the *St Patrick,* our ferry across the Irish Sea. Despite the chilly weather, we stood on the deck, feeling excited about the trip.

About five kilometres from the coast, we could no longer stay on deck. Gale-force winds were blowing, and we had to hold on to each other to avoid falling over. We struggled against the howling wind to the lounge below deck. We tried to drink some coffee, but the boat was pitching and rolling, so most of the coffee ended up on the floor. Huge waves were lashing against the windows and many people were heading for the bathroom, looking very queasy. We quickly forgot about our holiday plans, because we were paralysed with fear about ever reaching Ireland in one piece.

The ferry finally reached the coast of Ireland, but the storm had delayed us by three hours. We didn't enjoy the rest of the holiday, although Ireland was green and beautiful, because we were anxious about the return trip we would have to make across the sea!

b Complete the outline of the story in the table below. Some of the details have already been filled in.

Paragraph 1 – introduction	
	Feelings we had before the journey – excited
Paragraph 2 – main body	
	Feelings we had during the storm – paralysed with fear
Paragraph 3 – conclusion	
	Feelings we had during our holiday – anxious

6 Think about your introduction

a In the model text above, the writer sets the scene at the beginning of the story. Underline the answers to the following questions in the model text.

1 Who are the people in the story?
2 Where were they going?
3 When did the story happen?
4 Why were they travelling?
5 How were they travelling?
6 What was the weather like?

b The following extract is the second paragraph of a story. Write an introduction which answers the questions in **a**, and gives the reader an idea of the situation.

As we were driving along, it suddenly happened. The front tyre burst, and we had to stop on the edge of the road to get out to change it. Unfortunately, the spare tyre was also flat! Suddenly the sky turned black. Within seconds, we were all completely wet through. We sat inside the car, but the rain continued to pour down, and it still hadn't stopped an hour later. John decided he would try and walk to the nearest village to get help.

tip

Your introduction should include the background information your reader needs to understand how the story happened. A good way to do this is to answer the questions: Who? When? Where? Why? How?

7 Think about tenses
Tenses in stories
a Look at the following verbs from the final paragraph of the model text.

Past Perfect	Past Simple	Future in the Past
had delayed = flashback ◄———	reached	
	were anxious ———————►	would have to make = flash forward

Tenses in stories

Use the Past Perfect to talk about an event which happened before another event in the past. Use the Future in the Past to talk about an event which comes later in the story.

b Complete the following true story about Nicholas Scotti, the least successful tourist in the world, with the correct form of the verb in brackets.

The least successful tourist is Mr Nicholas Scotti of San Francisco. In 1977, he flew from America to his native Italy to visit relatives.

On the way, the plane made a one-hour stop at New York. He (1) .... (think) that he (2) .... (arrive) in Italy, and got out of the plane and spent two days in New York, thinking he was in Rome.

When his relatives were not there to meet him, Mr Scotti (3) .... (assume) that they (4) .... (delay) because of the heavy traffic, and that they (5) .... (turn up) soon. While he was looking for their address on a city map, he (6) .... (notice) that many of the famous ancient monuments (7) .... (disappear). He decided to try and find his family himself, but he (8) .... (be) worried that he (9) .... (get) lost, so he asked a policeman for help. The policeman happened to speak perfect Italian.

Even when he was told he was not in Rome, Mr Scotti refused to believe it. When the police were driving him back to the airport to catch the next plane home, he (10) .... (look) at the New York traffic and said, 'I know I'm in Italy. That's how they drive!'

8 Think about connectors
a Look at the following sentences from the model text on p.65. Underline the word in each sentence which introduces a contrast.

Despite the chilly weather, we stood on the deck, feeling excited about the trip.

We didn't enjoy the rest of the holiday, although Ireland was green and beautiful, because we were anxious about the return trip we would have to make across the sea!

b Some of the following sentences are incorrect. Put a tick (✓) by the correct sentences, and correct the others.

1 Despite of the traffic jam, I managed to get to the airport on time.

2 Although I had packed my case carefully, but I forgot my toothbrush.

3 Although Susan was tired after her trip, she went to work early the next day.

4 In spite of the strike, our plane took off on time.

5 Despite her suitcase was heavy, she carried it herself.

6 Although the heavy rain, we went out.

c Join the following pairs of sentences, first using *in spite of* or *despite,* and then using *although.*
(See **Writing Bank**, p.128.)

e.g. They went skiing. It was dangerous.

In spite of the danger, they went skiing.

Although it was dangerous, they went skiing.

1 The weather was dry. The country still looked green.

....

2 He was exhausted. He finished the race.

....

3 The waves were very high. I went swimming.

....

4 It was raining. We went to the park.

....

5 Lisa was ill. She didn't go to bed.

....

Exam practice: Write a story

You are going to write a story on the topic below. Do the tasks which follow.

You have received the following letter from a pen friend in Britain:

> Our college magazine is going to publish stories this month about journeys. We have been asked to find stories from around the world. Could you write a story for our magazine about a journey you made when the weather suddenly turned bad? I'll send you a copy of the magazine when it is published. I hope you can help!

Write your **story** (120–180 words).

- **Read the question**

  Read the question and underline the key words.

- **Think about paragraphing**

  Make an outline for your story.

- **Think about your introduction**

  Write your introduction with enough background for your reader to understand the situation.

- **Think about tenses**

  Make sure you use a range of tenses, and that you use them correctly.

- **Think about connectors**

  Link some sentences with *despite, in spite of* or *although.*

- **Edit your text**

  Check your writing for errors when you have finished.

Further practice

Write a story on the topic below.

> You have decided to enter a short story competition. The competition rules say that the story must begin with the following words: *I'll never forget the first time I travelled alone.*

Write your **story** for the competition (120–180 words).

15 A story beginning

1 Read the question

In Part 2 of the exam, you may be asked to write a story which starts in a certain way. You **must** use the words given and then continue the story. **Read the exam question below and underline the key words.**

> You have been asked to write a story for a student magazine beginning with these words: *Everybody was waiting. I felt nervous; this was going to be my first time on stage in a real theatre.*

Write your **story** (120–180 words).

2 Think about your reader

Work with a partner. Look at the exam question again and answer the following questions.

1 Your story will be printed in a student magazine. What kind of magazine might it be? Who might read this magazine? Decide this and write your answer according to your decision.

2 What would your reader expect to read about?

   a interesting information about life in the theatre

   b a vivid personal account of an experience

   c advice about pursuing a career in the theatre

   d a review of a play or a concert

3 Think about vocabulary

a Check you know the meaning of the words and expressions in the box.

> a leading role   a main part   a minor role   a piece of music
> a standing ovation   props   scenery   stage fright   to applaud   to cheer
> to clap   to dim the lights   to learn your lines   to rehearse   to take a bow

b Complete the following sentences using the words and expressions from **a**. Make any necessary changes. (Sometimes more than one answer is possible.)

1 We .... for months, so we all felt ready for the big night.

2 When they .... the stage lights, the audience fell silent.

3 I had only a .... in the play, so I didn't have a lot of .... to learn.

4 Did you see Mel Gibson in *Braveheart*? I thought he played the .... very well.

5 It was a very difficult .... to play, but I managed to play well.

6 At the end of the performance, the actors all came on stage together and ....

7 The performance was so moving, that the audience gave the actors ....

8 Everyone was involved in the play. The teachers painted all the background ...., and the parents supplied all the ....

9 It was my first leading role, and I was paralysed with ....

10 The audience .... and .... as their favourite singers came onto the stage.

4 Brainstorm the topic

a Work with a partner. Look at the extracts from the exam question on p.68 and answer the following questions. Make notes of any good ideas that you or your partner have.

1 *Everybody was waiting.*
- Who were they?
- Where were they exactly?
- What were they waiting for?
- Were they doing anything else while they were waiting?

2 *I felt nervous.*
- Why did you feel nervous?
- What thoughts went through your mind?
- How did you react physically?
- What did you try to do to stop yourself feeling nervous?

3 *This was going to be my first time on stage in a real theatre.*
- Why would you be going to perform on stage in a theatre?
- Have you ever been on stage in public? How did you feel before you began?
- Why would someone be nervous in this situation? Give examples of why someone gets nervous.
- Have you ever seen someone on stage who was really nervous? How did you know he/she was nervous?

b Use your notes from **a**, and choose a situation that you know something about from the table below. Work with a partner, and add some more ideas to one or both of the lists.

My first time on stage:	I thought I might:
playing in an orchestra	lose my place in the music drop my instrument
performing in a play	forget my words look silly
taking part in a public-speaking competition	make mistakes in the speech be unable to answer questions
performing a dance	fall over forget the steps
singing alone or with a group	sing when I should be silent drop my song sheet
receiving a prize for something	fall over on the steps forget to shake hands with the prize-giver

c The ideas in **a** and **b** should help you write the first part of your story. Think about the following aspects and decide how your story will continue.
- Will your stage performance be good, a disaster or a mixture of good and bad?
- Think of some things that could happen during the performance.
- Think about how you felt when it finished. What did your audience do? What did you do? What did the other people do?

5 Read a model text

a Read the following story. Was the writer's experience of being on stage positive, negative or a mixture of the two?

Everybody was waiting. I felt nervous; this was going to be my first time on a stage in a real theatre. In a few minutes, I was going to play my violin in public with our school orchestra. I was feeling sick with nerves, terrified that I would fall over or drop my instrument. Even worse was the feeling that I would disappoint my family and friends who had come to watch. I took a deep breath, walked onto the stage and sat down. At first, I was still trembling with nerves, but as we began to play, I gradually relaxed. Soon I forgot the audience and started to enjoy the music. It felt wonderful to be part of an orchestra, and I realised that all my months of practice had been worth it. At last, it was over, and the audience gave us a standing ovation. I had performed well, and I knew that I would never be nervous again. It was the best moment of my life.

b The model text in **a** has been written as a single paragraph, although it should have three paragraphs. Read it again, and decide where each paragraph should begin and end.

6 Link your text

a When you write a story, you should use time expressions to make the passing of time in the story clear to the reader. Look back at the model text and underline the time expressions which do this.

b Add the time expressions from the model text to the table below and any other examples you can think of.

Start of the story or action	Following parts of the story or action	Events that happened fast/ slowly	Events in the future of the story	End of the story or action

c Look at the following notes for the main events of two stories. Choose one of the sets of notes and write a short story, using time expressions to link your text.

Notes for story 1
- first time speaking in public
- very nervous
- lost my voice
- dropped my papers
- forgot to say thank you at the end
- fell when leaving the stage

Notes for story 2
- first time dancing on stage
- shaking with stage fright
- made a mistake, but nobody noticed
- relaxed, enjoyed it
- danced well
- audience gave standing ovation at end

7 Think about tenses

Future in the Past

a Imagine you are in the situation in the exam question. The performance begins in five minutes and you are waiting to go on stage. Read the following thoughts that are making you nervous now about the future. Underline the verbs in each one.

1 I'm afraid I will fall down on the stage.

2 I think that everyone will laugh at me.

3 I'm sure that I'll forget my part.

4 I'm terrified that I am going to make a mistake.

5 I think that I will drop my violin.

6 I'm scared I won't be very good.

7 I'm worried that the audience won't clap at the end.

8 I'm positive that I will disappoint my audience.

b When you write your story, you should use past tenses. Rewrite the sentences in **a** in the past.

e.g. *I was afraid I would fall down on the stage.*

> **Future in the Past**
>
> To talk about events in the future time of the story, use the Future in the Past.
> e.g. *In a few minutes, the bell **was going to ring**.*
> *Soon, the bell **would ring**.*

Exam practice: Write a story

You are going to write a story on the topic below. Do the tasks which follow.

> Your teacher has asked you to write a story for the school's English-language magazine. It must begin with the following words: *I had practised very hard for six months. Now it was time to see if I was really good enough.*

Write your **story** (120–180 words).

- **Read the question**

  Read the question and underline the key words.

- **Think about your reader**

  Identify the reader of your story and the style that you will use.

- **Brainstorm the topic**

  Make a list of all possibilities for your story, by asking yourself key questions, e.g.

  1 What had you been practising?

  2 Why had you been practising?

  3 *Now it was time* … What was going to happen?

- **Think about paragraphing**

  Make a list of ideas for the main events of the story, and decide how the story ends. Make an outline for your story with suitable paragraphs.

- **Link your text**

  Use suitable time expressions to show the sequence of events in your story.

- **Think about tenses**

  Use a range of tenses. Try to include some examples of Future in the Past.

- **Edit your text**

  Check your writing for errors when you have finished.

Further practice

Write a story on the topic below.

> You have decided to enter a short story competition. The competition rules say that the story must begin with the following words: *This was the moment we had all been waiting for. I took a deep breath and began.*

Write your **story** for the competition (120–180 words).

16 A story ending

1 Read the question

In Part 2 of the exam, you may be asked to write a story which ends in a certain way. You **must** use the words given. **Read the exam question below and underline the key words.**

> Your teacher has asked you to write a story for the school magazine.
> The story must end with the words:
> *Jane went home feeling very sorry for herself.*

Write your **story** (120–180 words).

2 Think about your reader

Work with a partner. Look at the exam question again and answer the following questions.

1 Who will read your story?

2 What style of writing should you use?

3 Brainstorm the topic

Work with a partner and answer the questions. (Sometimes more than one answer is possible.)

1 What kind of story could you write?

  a a happy story

  b a sad story

  c a story where both good and bad things happened

2 What could the story be about? Add more ideas to the following list.

- a story about a crime
- a story about an accident
- a story about a party
- a story about a relationship

3 Make notes on possible events for each of these stories.

- a crime
- a party
- an accident
- a relationship

4 Imagine what the main character in the story, Jane, is like. Think about her:

- age
- occupation
- family
- physical appearance
- character

4 Think about paragraphing

a Read the following story. What is strange about the way it is written?

Jane was in town one day with her friend, Marianna. They were shopping. They went into a clothes shop. Jane tried on a jacket. She took off her own jacket. She put her handbag on top of it. She decided to buy the jacket. She went to the cashier. She was waiting for her turn. The sales assistant told her that her bag was open. She quickly looked inside. She realised that her wallet had been stolen! Naturally, she panicked. She looked all over the shop. The wallet had disappeared. The manager offered to help her look for it. They didn't find it. She felt as if the end of the world had come. She was furious. She felt miserable at the same time. Her heart was beating fast. Her hands were shaking. A large amount of money had gone. She had also lost her credit and bank cards. Marianna suggested that they should go to the police. She went to the police station to report the theft. She knew she would never see her wallet again. Jane went home, feeling very sorry for herself.

b Mark where you think the paragraphs should begin and end in the story in **a**.

c Rewrite the sentences from the story in **a**, using linking words and making complex sentences with different kinds of clauses.

e.g. Jane was in town one day with her friend, Marianna. They were shopping. They went into a clothes shop. Jane tried on a jacket.

Jane was shopping in town one day, with her friend, Marianna. They went into a shop, where Jane tried on a jacket.

d The story in **a** would be more vivid if there were some examples of direct speech. Can you add two or three examples in suitable places in the story?

e Rewrite the story in **a**, with suitable paragraphs, complex sentences and direct speech.

5 Think about punctuation

Punctuate these examples of direct speech correctly.

1 please show me what you have in a size 10 she asked

2 can I try this on she asked

3 she said this is too big. have you got a smaller size

4 she screamed my wallet's been stolen

5 what does your wallet look like asked the manager

6 it's brown leather with a black zip she said

Punctuation in direct speech

- Open and close direct speech with quotation marks: '…' or "…"
- Write a capital letter for the first word in the direct speech: 'Do you like this jacket?'
- When the speech is introduced by a verb, put a comma after the verb: He said, '…'
- When the verb comes after the direct speech, put a comma, question mark or exclamation mark before the final quotation mark: '…,' she said.

---

6 Think about vocabulary

Describing feelings

Write the words and expressions in the box in the correct category.
(Some examples can fit in more than one category.)

A happy experience: ....

A sad experience: ....

An exciting experience: ....

A frightening experience: ....

---

dejected   delighted   despondent   distraught   downhearted   elated
exhilarated   overjoyed   petrified   scared stiff   terrified   thrilled

---

tip

If you have to write about a character in a story, build up a picture of the person first, and make notes about his/her age, occupation, family, etc. Add any relevant vocabulary to your notes that may be useful in your story.

7 Edit your text

a Each code in the table below tells you what kind of error the writer has made. Correct the underlined errors.

Code	Meaning	Example
WW	Wrong word	I <u>made</u> my homework.
WF	Correct word, but change the form.	I was very <u>interesting</u> in the book.
SP	Spelling error	I am <u>writting</u> to you …
P	Punctuation error	<u>Im</u> leaving tomorrow.
T	Tense error	I <u>have seen</u> him last week.
WO	Word order is wrong.	He likes <u>very much</u> chocolates.
X	In this line, cross out one word.	When I will finish, I'll call you.
^	Something is missing here.	I love listening ^ music.

b Correct the errors in the following story, using the error codes in **a**.

> One day, I decided ^{WF}<u>taking</u> my youngest sister to the circus. My sister was very ^{WF}<u>exciting</u> and she couldn't wait in the queue to buy our tickets. She ^{WW}<u>said</u> X me, 'John, I ^T<u>go</u> inside.' 'Wait! You can't to go in without a ticket!' I replied, but she didn't ^{WF}<u>heard</u> me.
>
> When I ^T<u>bought</u> the tickets, I thought that my sister ^T<u>will</u> be waiting ^ me at the entrance of the circus. I was wrong. I asked the man at the door, '^{WO}<u>You have</u> seen a little girl?' He said ^P<u>A</u> little girl ran past me and went inside.'
>
> I thanked him, and ^{WW}<u>got</u> inside to start looking for her.
>
> The show ^T<u>didn't start</u> yet, and I couldn't find her, ^{WW}<u>despite</u> I ^T<u>look</u> almost everywhere, even under the chairs. After a while, I remembered that she loved X the animals, and that when she ^T<u>grow</u> up, she ^T<u>want</u> to become ^ vet. So I thought that she might be with the animals at the back of the circus. I was very ^{SP}<u>releived</u> when I saw her ^{WF}<u>to laugh</u> with the monkeys. I said, 'Let's go inside and see the show.' She replied, 'I'd rather stay here and just see the animals!'
>
> In the end, she agreed to watch the show. But because I nearly lost her, when we got home, we didn't tell anyone about what had happened.

8 Think about grammar

Reporting verbs

a Look at the following examples from the story in **4 Think about paragraphing a** and underline the reporting verbs.

The sales assistant told her that her bag was open.

The manager offered to help her look for it.

b Look at the reporting verbs in the box below.

1 Which verbs are followed by a *that* clause? Put a tick (✓) beside these verbs.

2 Which verbs are followed by *to do* (an infinitive)? Write *I*.

3 Which verbs are followed by *-ing* (a gerund)? Write *G*.

4 Write the correct preposition next to the appropriate verbs.

> accuse admit advise agree apologise ask deny encourage explain
> offer promise refuse say suggest tell warn

c Rewrite the following sentences in reported speech, using the best reporting verb from the box in **b** on p.74 for the context given. Do not use *say, tell* or *ask*. Use a different verb in each sentence.

1 'You stole my wallet!' I said to the sales assistant.

....

2 'I didn't steal your money!' said the sales assistant.

....

3 'My advice is to go to the police,' Marianna said.

....

4 'Why don't you look in that plastic bag?' said Marianna.

....

5 'OK. I *did* steal your wallet,' the sales assistant said.

....

6 'No! I won't do it!' Jane said.

....

7 'I'm sorry I didn't keep an eye on your bag,' Marianna said.

....

8 'Don't ever leave your bag open again,' my father said.

....

Exam practice: Write a story

You are going to write a story on the topic in the advertisement opposite. Do the tasks which follow.

You have seen this advertisement in a magazine, and you decide to enter the competition.

Write your **story** for the competition (120–180 words).

- **Read the question**

  Read the question carefully and underline the key words. Should you use the words given at the end of the story or at the beginning? Or, do you have a choice?

- **Think about your reader**

  Who is going to read your story?

- **Brainstorm the topic**

  Imagine who your character is, and build up a picture of him. What situation could he be in? Look at the words you must use, and think of a suitable situation.

- **Think about paragraphing**

  Make notes for the events of the story, and develop an outline. Make sure you use appropriate paragraphs, write an introduction that gives the background to the story, and a conclusion that ends the story in a good way. Remember not to change the words given.

Short story competition!

Prizes for the best five stories!

Write a short story for *English Now!* magazine, and win valuable prizes. The only rule is that you must end your story with these words:

Peter put down his pen, and turned to answer her, but she had gone.

Send your stories to:

English Now!
143, Havilland Avenue
Manchester M16 6TQ
England

- **Think about grammar**

  Try to use a range of tenses including Past Continuous, Past Perfect and Future in the Past. Use direct speech in your story where appropriate.

- **Edit your text**

  Check your writing for errors when you have finished.

Further practice

Write a story on the topic below.

> You have decided to enter a short story competition. The competition rules say that the story must begin or end with the following words:
> *James switched on the light and sat down at his desk.*

Write your **story** for the competition (120–180 words).

17 Discussing pros and cons

1 Read the question

In Part 2 of the exam, you are often asked to write a discursive composition, which can be on a range of topics. **Read the exam question below and underline the key words.**

> You have had a class discussion on school exams. Your teacher has now asked you to write a composition with the following title:
> *Taking exams has both positive and negative effects on students.*

Write your **composition** (120–180 words).

exam tip

There are different types of discursive composition in Part 2 of the exam. You can be asked to:

- give a balanced argument on a topic. This means discussing the pros and cons of a situation or statement.
- give your opinion on a topic.
- make suggestions about a topic or problem.

Make sure you read the question carefully and that you understand what type of answer you are expected to give.

2 Think about your reader

Work with a partner. Look at the exam question again and answer the following questions.

1 Who is going to read your composition?

2 Which style of writing will you use for your reader?
  a very informal
  b quite formal
  c chatty and colloquial

3 What format do you need to use?
  a letter format
  b a story
  c paragraphed text with no specific format
  d report format
  e newspaper article format

4 Which of the following outlines for the composition is the most appropriate?

a
1 Introduction
2 Positive and negative effects of exams
3 Solutions to the problems exams cause
4 Conclusion

b
1 Introduction
2 The positive effects of taking exams
3 The negative effects of taking exams
4 Conclusion

c
1 Introduction
2 The problems exams cause
3 Ways to cope with the problems
4 Conclusion

d
1 Introduction
2 Advantages of exams in school
3 My personal opinions on exams
4 Conclusion

3 Brainstorm the topic

Work with a partner and answer the questions.

1 How do you feel when you take an exam?

2 How do some people react during exams? What do they do?

3 Do you think there is an alternative way of assessing students, other than taking exams? What could be done instead?

4 Discuss the different effects of taking exams with your partner. Make notes in the table below.

	Positive effects	Negative effects
The students' state of mind		
The subject they have been studying		
The students' physical state		
Other ideas		

4 Read a model text

Read the model text and complete the outline for paragraphs 2 and 3 in the table below.

Most teachers believe that exams have advantages over other ways of assessing students' progress. However, taking exams usually fills most of us with dread.

Exams can indeed have beneficial results. First of all, an exam forces students to revise all the work covered in the school year. As a result, they regain valuable knowledge that may have been forgotten. In addition, exams are an effective way of preparing students for the stressful situations that they may meet in their future working life.

On the other hand, exams can have negative effects. Many students cannot handle stress very well, and consequently may not be able to perform at their best. This, in turn, produces exam results that are not a fair reflection of the student's true ability. Another negative effect is that students may revise very hard for a short time before the exam, and then forget everything the minute the exam is over.

I believe that exams are necessary, but should not be the only way to determine a student's future. I think a combination of exams and continual assessment of work is a fairer method.

Main topic of paragraph	Topic sentence	Details
2		
3		

17 Discussing pros and cons

5 Think about your introduction and conclusion

a Look back at the model text on p.77 and read the introduction again. What is the writer trying to do in the introduction?

1 say how much students hate exams

2 establish the general topic for the composition

3 talk about the negative effects of exams

b Read the conclusion to the model text again. What is the writer trying to do in the conclusion?

1 strongly recommend exams

2 strongly criticise exams

3 give a balanced personal comment on the topic

c Look at the following composition titles. Write a suitable introduction and conclusion for one of the titles.

1 Owning a motorbike. A death trap or a good way to travel?

2 The advantages and disadvantages of living in a big city

tip

For discursive compositions giving a balanced argument:

1 State the general topic in the first paragraph.

2 Discuss the pros of the statement or situation, giving two or three supporting details.

3 Discuss the cons of the statement or situation, giving two or three supporting details.

4 Put a personal comment in the conclusion.

6 Think about connectors

a The writer of the model text uses different words and phrases to link the text together. Look back at the model text on p.77 and find the following examples.

1 Underline the words and phrases that are used to introduce an opposite idea.

2 Underline the words and phrases that are used to show an additional idea.

3 Underline the words and phrases that are used to show a result.

b Look back at the two topics in **5 Think about your introduction and conclusion c**. Choose one of these topics and make a list of ideas for the main paragraphs. Write the two main paragraphs, including suitable linking words and phrases.

7 Think about grammar
Omission of the definite article

a In discursive writing, you often need to refer to things in general. Look at the following examples from the model text.

*Most teachers believe that **exams** have advantages …*

*In addition, **exams** are an effective way of preparing **students** for **the stressful situations** that they may meet in their future working life.*

The words in **bold** show the writer's use or omission of the article *the*. Why is the article missing in all the examples except one?

b Read the following extract from a composition about scientific experiments on animals. Correct the mistakes in the use of the article.

As some of us know, experimenting on the animals gives benefits to the humans, but harms animals a great deal. Currently, the science has made everything possible. By turning theory into reality, the scientists have found useful cures for those patients who may never have had the hope of being healthy. For example, patients who had the cancer, thanks to the new technology, are healthy. Another great achievement is in the treatment of the hereditary diseases. Cures have been found after the scientists located the genes which cause them. Such efforts are also being made for the diabetes and the obesity. At the same time, while people are being cured, many animals are suffering in the laboratories. Just because the man is more important than the animals, it doesn't mean that we can do whatever we like.

Exam practice: Write a composition

You are going to write a composition on the topic below. Do the tasks which follow.

You have had a class discussion about the following statement:
Women should stay at home and look after children.
Your teacher has now asked you to write a composition, discussing points for and against the statement.

Write your **composition** (120–180 words).

- **Read the question**

  Read the question and underline the key words.

- **Think about your reader**

  Identify your reader, and a suitable style for your answer.

- **Think about paragraphing**

  Make an outline for your answer, using the guide on p.76.

- **Think about connectors**

  Include linking words and phrases to make your ideas clear to your reader.

- **Edit your text**

  Check your writing for errors when you have finished.

Further practice

Write a composition on the topic below.

You have been doing a class project on TV programmes. Your teacher has asked you to write a composition with the following title:
The benefits and drawbacks to watching TV.

Write your **composition** (120–180 words).

18 Giving your opinion (1)

1 Read the question

In Part 2 of the exam, you may be asked to write a composition giving your own opinion on a topic, or to give your opinion and examples from your personal experience. **Read the exam question below and underline the key words.**

> The following comment was printed recently in a local newspaper:
> *Schools should teach our young people useful practical skills, and not just boring academic subjects.*
> Now your teacher has asked you to write a composition on this subject, with reference to your own learning experience.

Write your **composition** (120–180 words).

2 Think about your reader

Work with a partner. Look at the exam question again and answer the following questions. (Sometimes more than one answer is possible.)

1 Who is going to read your composition?

2 Which style of writing will you use for your reader?

3 What format do you need to use?

4 Which of the following could you do in your composition?

    a agree with the comment

    b add examples from your own experience

    c disagree with the comment

    d agree with the comment up to a point

    e describe your favourite teacher

    f discuss the advantages and disadvantages of learning academic subjects

    g disagree with the comment up to a point

    h argue both sides of the subject in the comment

> **exam tip**
>
> When the exam task asks for your opinion, decide how you feel about the statement and choose a suitable approach. You can:
>
> - agree
> - partly agree
> - disagree
> - partly disagree
> - write a balanced argument if you accept both sides of the statement

3 Think about vocabulary

School subjects

a Answer the following questions, using the words in the box.

> Art Biology Chemistry Design Technology Drama English French Geography
> German Greek History Home Economics Information Technology
> Latin Maths Music Physical Education Physics Religious Studies Spanish

1 What are the three science subjects?

2 What do/did you do for Physical Education?

3 What do you think you learn in Home Economics, Design Technology and Information Technology?

4 What Arts subjects do/did you study?

5 Did you learn/are you learning any other subjects?

b Look at the following examples and decide which is correct.

1 *Maths is difficult.* OR *Maths are difficult.*

2 *French is easy.* OR *French are easy.*

Practical skills

Work with a partner. Look at the list of practical skills (sometimes called *life skills*) that are important for young people. Add more examples to the list.

- knowing how to cook
- knowing how to sew
- managing money

4 Brainstorm the topic

Work with a partner and answer the questions.

1 What are the benefits of learning academic subjects and more practical subjects? Add more ideas to the lists in the table below.

Academic subjects	Practical subjects
• provide a good, all-round education	• give guidance with careers
• train students to analyse	• equip students with life skills
	• have practical value in an adult world

2 What subjects do you/did you study at school? Are they useful in everyday life?

3 Are the following subjects useful in adult life? Why (not)?

- Latin
- Maths
- Chemistry
- History
- Geography
- English

4 Which practical skills would you like to see taught in schools?

5 After your discussion, do you agree or disagree with the statement in the exam question on p.80?

5 Read a model text

Read the model text and answer the following questions.

1 Does the writer agree or disagree with the statement in the exam question? Underline the expression that states this.

2 What is the main idea in paragraphs 2, 3 and 4?

3 How does the writer conclude the composition?

I couldn't agree more that schools do not teach enough practical skills. Many young people leave school with good general knowledge, but have no idea how to survive in an adult world.

One important skill schools should teach is how to succeed in a job interview, so that school leavers can feel confident about applying for their first job. My first job interview only exposed my inadequacies, and I failed to get the job.

Boys as well as girls should be taught how to cook and sew. As a result, young people will not suffer the shock of coping alone when they leave home. I, for example, was grateful for my Home Economics lessons during my first weeks at university.

Another important skill is learning how to manage money, so that young people don't spend their grant or salary all at once. My first pay cheque disappeared in only one week, and I immediately had to borrow. Consequently, I was always trying to repay my debts.

If young people were taught more practical skills like these, I believe that they would get a better start in their adult life.

18 Giving your opinion (1)

6 Think about paragraphing

a Look back at paragraph 2 in the model text on p.81. Underline the following three ideas in the paragraph, using different colour pens (red for the main idea, blue for the result and black for the personal example).

- a main idea
- a result of the main idea
- an example from personal experience

b Look at paragraphs 3 and 4 in the model text. Underline the main ideas, the results and examples of personal experience.

c Make an outline for a composition which disagrees with the statement in the exam question on p.80. Remember to use the pattern shown in **a**.

7 Link your text

a Look back at the model text. Underline the words and phrases which express a result.

b Write a result for each of the following ideas. Use a different word or phrase for each sentence.

1 Everybody must go to school.

....

2 Sports lessons are necessary every week.

....

3 Our teacher was very patient and encouraging.

....

4 Students should study hard for tests.

....

5 The school thinks it is very important to teach Music.

....

> **Showing results**
>
> This means …   Consequently, …
> …, so that …   If + past, … would
> As a result, …   + infinitive

8 Think about language

Expressing an opinion

a Look at the following sentences and underline the words that introduce an opinion.

1 I completely agree that schools do not teach enough practical skills.

2 I believe that all schools should train students to be responsible adults.

3 In my opinion, learning Latin is a waste of time.

4 I strongly disagree with the statement.

5 I think that I had a very good education, although I studied only academic subjects.

6 As far as I am concerned, Physical Education is very important.

7 In my view, education should be as broad as possible.

b Read the following sentences that express agreement and disagreement. Which ones express:

- strong agreement?   • strong disagreement?   • partial agreement?

1 I couldn't agree more with the statement.

2 I agree with the statement up to a point.

3 I completely agree with the statement.

4 I agree with the statement to a certain extent.

5 I am totally against the idea of …

6 I cannot see one point in favour of this statement.

7 It is clear that there are two sides to this statement.

c Write sentences, giving your opinion on the following statements. Use a different expression from **a** or **b** in each sentence.

1 Girls and boys should be educated separately.

....

2 Everyone should study one ancient language.

....

3 Education is more important than earning money.

....

4 The compulsory school-leaving age should be 18.

....

5 English should be a compulsory school subject at all ages.

....

Exam practice: Write a composition

You are going to write a composition on the topic below. Do the tasks which follow.

> Your class has been discussing the following statement: *Studying Music, Art and Drama is a waste of time.* Your teacher now wants you to write a composition, giving your opinion on the statement, and referring to your own learning of these subjects.

Write your **composition** (120–180 words).

- **Read the question**

  Read the question and underline the key words. Decide if you agree or disagree with the statement.

- **Think about your reader**

  Identify your reader, and a suitable style for your answer.

- **Make a plan**

  Make an outline for your composition:

  1 Introduction: state your opinion

  2 Main paragraphs: write one idea in each paragraph, show a result of the main idea, and add an example from personal experience

  3 Conclusion: summarise your ideas

- **Edit your text**

  Check your writing for errors when you have finished.

Further practice

Write a composition on the topic below.

> Your class has been reading a text about English as an international language. The title of the text was: *English is the only foreign language worth learning.* Your teacher now wants you to write a composition, giving your opinion on this subject.

Write your **composition** (120–180 words).

19 Giving your opinion (2)

1 Read the question

In Part 2 of the exam, you may be asked to give your opinion on a topic such as the environment, teenage life, education, entertainment, etc. **Read the exam question below and underline the key words. Use the question which follows to help you.**

> Your teacher has asked you to write a composition, giving your opinion on the following statement:
> *Young people should do sports in their free time, and not waste their lives watching TV and playing computer games.*

Write your **composition** (120–180 words).

What does the statement in the exam question really mean?

a Young people should stop watching TV and playing computer games, and do sports instead.

b Young people should divide their time between sports and their TV or computer.

c Young people should spend their free time with their TV or computer, instead of doing sports.

2 Think about your reader

Work with a partner. Look at the exam question again and answer the following questions.

1 Who is going to read your composition?

2 Which style of writing will you use for your reader?

3 What format do you need to use?

3 Think about vocabulary

Sports and outdoor activities

a Work with a partner. Make a list of all the sports and outdoor activities that you do, or that you have done in the past.

b Look at the activities in the box and decide if they are used with *go, do* or *play*.

go: ....

do: ....

play: ....

> athletics   basketball   bowling   cycling   fishing   football   gymnastics   hockey   outdoor activities
> parachuting   sailing   skating   sports   swimming   snowboarding   volleyball   windsurfing

Benefits of leisure activities

a Look at the list of benefits and decide if they come from doing sports (S), playing computer games (CG) or watching television (TV). Sometimes more than one answer is possible.

- develop muscular strength   *S*
- improve circulation
- improve hand–eye co-ordination
- increase mental alertness
- help cope with stress
- provide an outlet for excess energy
- develop social skills

- build team spirit
- give access to information
- broaden education
- improve problem-solving skills
- increase awareness of the world
- provide a break from studying

b Add any other benefits you can think of for each activity.

4 Brainstorm the topic

Work with a partner and answer the questions.

1 What activities do you do in your free time? What benefits do you gain from them?

2 What are the possible disadvantages of spending *all* your free time either doing sports, watching TV or playing computer games?

3 Do you think that young people in your country spend too much time in front of the TV or playing computer games? If so, what are the reasons for this?

4 After your discussion, do you agree or disagree with the statement in the exam question?

5 Read a model text

a Read the model text and answer the following questions.

1 Does the writer agree or disagree with the statement in the exam question? Underline the part(s) of the text where the writer states an opinion(s).

2 Are the main ideas organised into logical paragraphs?

3 What does the writer do in the introduction and in the conclusion?

I agree with the statement to a certain extent, as I believe physical fitness is important. However, watching TV and playing computer games are not necessarily harmful.

Watching a reasonable amount of TV can have some benefits. One main advantage is that TV can inform and educate if the programmes are chosen carefully. The news, for example, brings the outside world into our homes, and young people are kept abreast of world events. In addition, documentaries can provide valuable educational input for children still at school.

Computer games also have some positive effects. First of all, children can become familiar with modern technology, which will have practical value for their future careers. In addition, computer games also train hand–eye co-ordination, provide enjoyment and a break from studying.

In my view, our lives should have a good balance between exercise and relaxation. If schools do not have a good physical education programme, children should be encouraged to take exercise, such as aerobics or swimming, and not be left to sit in front of the TV or playing computer games every day.

b Write a brief summary of each paragraph in the spaces below.

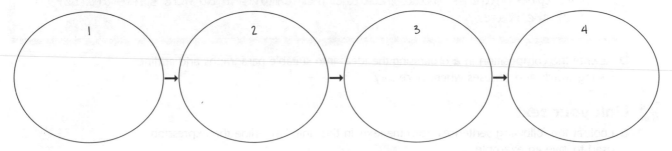

c The composition below is an answer to the same exam question on p.84, but some parts of it are missing. Complete the composition with any suitable word(s).

I completely disagree with the statement. Many young people today have too
.... in their busy school life, so TV and computer games are a
good way ....

Computer games and TV programmes offer many benefits. One important
example is .... For example, I saw a computer game where
....

In addition to the benefits offered by computer games, TV has its advantages, too.
Many programmes are ...., such as ....

As far as I am concerned, young people should spend their leisure time
.... This means that they will ....

In addition, they can .... Parents should also
....

6 Think about paragraphing

a Read the first draft of a composition a student wrote to answer the exam question on p.84. Are the main ideas organised into logical paragraphs?

I couldn't agree more that TV programmes and computer games have bad effects on the youth of today. They encourage them to sit motionless for hours, so that they become unhealthy through lack of exercise. Television today is full of rubbish. For instance, I have 25 channels and they all show stupid game shows and American police stories. Computer games are violent and pointless. A healthy sport such as cycling or basketball would develop the mind as well as the body. Young people spend far too long staring at the screen until three or four o'clock in the morning, so that they are too tired to study in school the next day. Parents don't care what TV programmes they watch, and children frequently see things intended only for an adult audience. One example of a particularly mindless computer game is where a monkey has to collect as many bananas as possible. Another requires the player to kill as many soldiers as possible in a certain time. In my opinion, parents should encourage their children to do more sports and get out of the house.

b Rewrite the composition in **a** organising the ideas into suitable paragraphs and adding linking words and phrases where necessary.

7 Link your text

a Look at the following sentences from the texts in this unit. Underline the expressions used to give an example.

For example, I saw a computer game where …

… children should be encouraged to take exercise, such as aerobics or swimming …

For instance, I have 25 channels and they all show stupid game shows …

One example of a particularly mindless computer game is …

b Read the following general statements. Write a specific example or examples to follow each statement, using the expressions in the box below.

e.g. A lot of TV programmes are educational. *For instance, National Geographic programmes can teach children a lot about nature.*

1 There is a lot of rubbish on television.

....

2 I believe that young people should do more sports.

....

3 I have tried many water sports.

....

4 Some of the best computer games are non-violent.

....

5 There is a lot of violence on the news.

....

Giving examples

Giving examples is a good way to make your writing more specific.
Use the following expressions:

For example, …   …, such as …
For instance, …   One example of … is …

Exam practice: Write a composition

You are going to write a composition on the topic below. Do the tasks which follow.

You have had a class discussion on the following statement:
Teenagers should get a part-time job to learn how to become responsible adults.
Your teacher would now like you to write a composition, giving your opinion on the statement.

Write your **composition** (120–180 words).

● **Read the question**

Read the question and underline the key words. Decide if you agree or disagree with the statement.

● **Think about your reader**

Identify your reader, and a suitable style for your answer.

● **Make a plan**

Make notes for your composition, giving examples to support your opinions.

● **Think about paragraphing**

Organise your ideas into paragraphs. State your opinion clearly in your introduction. Write a clear topic sentence for each main paragraph. Write a conclusion summarising your overall opinion.

● **Edit your text**

Check your writing for errors when you have finished.

Further practice

Write a composition on the topic below.

Your teacher has asked you to write a composition, giving your opinion on the following statement:
People should work or study less and play more.

Write your **composition** (120–180 words).

20 Suggesting solutions

1 Read the question

In Part 2 of the exam, you may be asked to give your opinion on a topic, and suggest solutions to problems. **Read the exam question below and underline the key words. Use the questions which follow to help you.**

> Your class has been doing a project on 'Animals in Danger'. Your teacher would now like you to write a composition to answer the following questions:
> *What can ordinary people do to protect endangered species? What do you think is the best way for them to do this?*

Write your **composition** (120–180 words).

1 Which question in the exam task asks for your suggestions?

2 Which question in the exam task asks for your opinion?

2 Think about your reader

Work with a partner. Look at the exam question again and answer the following questions.

1 Who is going to read your composition?

2 Which style of writing will you use for your reader?

3 What format do you need to use?

3 Think about vocabulary

a The exam question contains the terms *Animals in danger* and *endangered species*. Complete the following ways of expressing the same idea in different words.

1 Many animals today are threatened with ....

2 Many animals today are .... out.

3 Many animals are becoming ....

b Why are animals in danger? Put the words in the box in the correct category.

Hunting: ....

Threats to habitat: ....

Pollution: ....

| farming forest clearance fur housing industrial waste ivory mining |
| motorways over-fishing sewerage skins whale oil |

c What can be done to protect endangered species? Complete the following text with the words from the box.

| ban charities donate join laws lobby |

In order to protect endangered species, we can (1) .... environmental organisations, such as Friends of the Earth. We can also (2) .... money to other conservation (3) .... We can try to (4) .... Members of Parliament, so that they will introduce (5) .... which (6) .... the sale of products from animals in danger of extinction.

4 Brainstorm the topic

Work with a partner and answer the questions.

1 Which animal do you think is most in need of protection?

2 How is it possible to help endangered species in your country?

3 Do you do anything to support the protection of endangered species?

4 What do you think is the best way that an ordinary person could help?

5 Compare two model texts

a Read the two model texts below and say which you think is better and why.
Use the checklist below to help you.

- Does the composition include all the points asked for in the exam question?
- Does each paragraph have one clear topic?
- Does each paragraph have a clear topic sentence, where necessary?
- Does the writer use linking words and phrases to make the meaning clear?
- Does the introduction give the reader an overall idea of the composition?
- Does the conclusion summarise the whole composition, or make a personal comment?

Model text 1

Everyone can and should make an effort to help protect endangered species.

Wc should never buy products made from animals in danger. All sales of fur coats should be banned, and it should be considered bad taste to wear even an old one.

We need to make young people aware of the dangers facing this planet before it is too late.

We can try to influence local politicians, so that they will help to pass laws preventing hunting, pollution and the cutting down of forests.

Schools should make sure that Ecology is a compulsory subject, so that children know about the issues, and will grow up with a conservationist attitude.

Nobody should want to own anything made of ivory or alligator skin.

Children are the future, and they will live in a world with less diversity in wildlife than at any other time in the past, if we do not do something now.

We can join a wildlife protection organisation, and help to publicise the problems, by putting up posters in schools and public places, and organising fund-raising activities.

Model text 2

It is one of the great disasters of this century that people have slowly managed to destroy certain species by hunting, pollution and forest clearance. I believe that ordinary people can and should do something, however small, to help protect endangered species.

One example of action that we can take is to join a local conservation group, and get involved in the activities that the group organises. For example, we could offer to talk to schools about the problem of endangered animals in the local area. Furthermore, we should absolutely refuse to buy anything that contains animal products from endangered species, such as fur coats, alligator skin shoes or cosmetics made from whale oil. Donating money to charities which work to protect animals in danger of extinction, like the World Wildlife Fund, is something we can all do.

In my view, the best way for ordinary people to help endangered species is education. If schools gave lessons which raised awareness of the problems, children would understand, perhaps better than adults, that their own future is going to be bleak without a rich variety of wildlife on the planet.

20 Suggesting solutions

b Rewrite **Model text 1** so that:

- it has good paragraph organisation.
- it has a good conclusion.
- it states the best way to protect endangered species, as asked for in the exam question.
- it includes linking words and phrases.

6 Think about your introduction

a Look back at the two sentences in the introduction to **Model text 2** on p.89. Which sentence:

1 gives a general background to the topic?

2 introduces the main point of the composition, as asked for in the exam question?

b Write an introductory paragraph, giving general background and introducing the main point, for the following topic.

What do you think is the best transport to protect the environment?

7 Edit your text

a Look at the following first draft of a composition that a student wrote. Correct the errors in the text. If necessary, look at the error codes list on p.74 to help you.

> Many people **thinks** [WF] that the problem of protecting the environment is ˄concern of the government, but I believe that ordinary people can do **anything** [WW] too.
> I think that we can give money to a charity that it protects the **enviroment.** [SP]   X
> Our donations can help to change things, however small **it** [WW] may be.
> In addition, we must stop killing wild animals and **destroy** [WF] the nature. We can   X
> join a local organisation and take part in **it's** activities.
> Furthermore, there are many other problems that we must solve them. People   X
> can help reduce pollution by walking or taking the bus to work every day instead
> of **drive** [WF] their cars. **Except** [WW] this, we can try to drive only when ˄is absolutely
> necessary.
> We should all try to protect the environment, because if we continue to damage
> the Earth, our children **hadn't** [T] **nowhere** [WW] to live.

b The writer of the text in **a** has used relatively simple structures and vocabulary. Rewrite the text, using more sophisticated language, so that the composition would get a higher mark.

e.g. I think that we can give money to a charity that protects the environment.

Donating money to a charity that protects the environment is one example of action that we can take.

---

exam tip

Remember to keep checking your writing for errors as you go along. In the exam, leave yourself enough time to check your answers to both Parts 1 and 2 carefully.

Exam practice: Write a composition

You are going to write a composition on the topic below. Do the tasks which follow.

> Your teacher has asked you to write a composition which answers the
> following question:
> *What can we do to help reduce air pollution? What do you think is the best way to
> do this?*

Write your **composition** (120–180 words).

- **Read the question**

  Read the question and underline the key words.

- **Think about your reader**

  Identify your reader, and a suitable style for your answer.

- **Think about vocabulary**

  Note down useful vocabulary before you start to write.

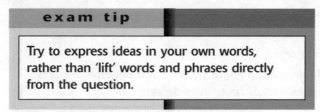

> **exam tip**
>
> Try to express ideas in your own words,
> rather than 'lift' words and phrases directly
> from the question.

- **Think about paragraphing**

  Write an introduction, giving a general background to the topic. In the main paragraphs,
  write suggestions for different solutions to the problem. In the conclusion, write your opinion
  on the best way to handle the problem. Use the writing checklist on p.89 to help you.

- **Edit your text**

  Check your writing for errors when you have finished.

Further practice

Write a composition on the topic below.

> You have been discussing the topic 'Today, we throw away too much rubbish'.
> Your teacher would like you to write a composition on the subject with the
> following title:
> *What can we do to recycle waste? What do you think is the best way to do this?*

Write your **composition** (120–180 words).

21 Evaluating places

1 Read the question

In Part 2 of the exam, you may be asked to write a report which evaluates places, events, arrangements, etc. **Read the exam question below and underline the key words.**

> You have recently started work in a local travel company, and you had to visit a new tourist attraction (for example, a museum, a nightclub or a park) in your area. Now you must write a report for your boss.

Write your **report** (120–180 words), describing the attraction, what it has to offer to tourists and commenting on its good and bad points.

exam tip

If you choose the report option in Part 2 of the exam, it's important to remember the key features of report-writing:

- Reports are usually written for someone in authority (your boss, the head of a school, etc.)
- Reports are always formal in style.
- Reports usually state factual information about positive and negative aspects of a place, etc. and make suggestions or recommendations.

2 Think about your reader

Work with a partner. Look at the exam question again and answer the following questions. (Sometimes more than one answer is possible.)

1 Who is going to read your report?

2 Which style of writing will you use for your reader?

3 Which of the following options could you write about? Which of the options are inappropriate, and why?

  a a well-known museum, nightclub or park

  b a new beach club in your area

  c a world-famous tourist attraction in your area that draws huge crowds every year

  d the new underground transport system in your city

  e a new museum, nightclub or park in your area

4 What will your reader expect you to do?

  a describe the attraction generally, highlight the aspects that would appeal to tourists, and report on its positive and negative points

  b describe the attraction and say how it benefits local people

  c describe the good and bad points of the attraction

  d describe your visit to the attraction in great detail, and say why you liked it

3 Brainstorm the topic

Work with a partner and answer the questions.

1 Choose a tourist attraction in your country or area, and make a list of its facilities.

  e.g. *café, children's play area*

2 What makes it especially good for tourists?

  e.g. *information office, staff speak different languages*

3 What are the good points and the bad points of the attraction?

  e.g. *good – efficient transport to the city, beautiful setting; bad – high prices, closes early*

4 Think about format and style

Look at the extracts below and say which one is a report. What features of the text gave you the answer?

1

The newest place in town!

Relax on the beach at the luxurious Tropicana Beach Club, under the shade of tropical umbrellas, and be served by friendly waiters. The sea is a sparkling blue, the beach has beautiful white sand, and all you need is close by – a bar, showers, toilets, and a restaurant.

2

The purpose of this document is to assess the new Tropicana Beach Club's suitability for tourists.

General information

The Club is situated 5 km. from the city centre, and can be easily reached by bus, tram or taxi. It is open daily from 8.30 a.m. to midnight during the summer season. The entrance fee is £5.00 for adults, £3.00 for children and students.

Facilities

There is a restaurant, a bar, showers and toilets. Umbrellas and tables are provided on the beach, with waiter service. Wind-surfers, jet skis, and small sailing boats can be hired.

3

I thought we could try the new Tropicana Beach Club that has just opened. I've heard that it's quite expensive, but the beach and the sea are fantastic, and it has showers, toilets and a restaurant. We could spend the whole day relaxing by the sea and you could rest after your flight.

tip

Make sure you include the following features in any report:

- formal style
- relatively short sentences with few clauses
- full verb forms
- impersonal language, e.g. passive verb forms
- headings and numbering to divide the information clearly

5 Think about vocabulary

Rewrite the following sentences to make them suitable for a formal report, using the words and phrases in the box. Make any necessary changes.

e.g. I want to tell you if it's good for tourists or not.

This report is to assess its suitability for tourists.

1 You pay when you get there.

....

2 You can buy drinks from the bar.

....

3 You can find the club just before the Grand Hotel.

....

4 You pay £5 to get in.

....

5 Lots of people would like it.

....

6 I think it's a really good place.

....

7 It's easy to get to from town.

....

8 If you go in a group, you can get in cheaper.

....

available   located   on arrival   reduced rates
strongly recommend   the entrance fee
within easy reach   would appeal to

21 Evaluating places

6 Read a model text

Read the model text and answer the following questions.

1 Does the report contain all the points asked for in the exam question?

2 Has the writer used the correct format and style?

3 Would the reader be able to get the information they need easily? Why?

tip

When you write a report, you don't need to write topic sentences for your paragraphs. You can write paragraph headings instead, with the details of the paragraph as numbered points.

To: Ms Tania Markus
From: Alexandra Barrett
Date: 15 September 199-
Subject: New attractions – Tropicana Beach Club

Introduction
As requested, this report is to assess the suitability of the new Tropicana Beach Club for tourists.

General information
The Club is situated 5 km. from the city, and can be easily reached by public transport. It is open daily from 8.30 a.m. to midnight during the summer. The entrance fee is £5.00 for adults, £3.00 for children and students.

Facilities
There is a restaurant, a bar, showers and toilets. Umbrellas and tables are provided on the beach, with waiter service. Wind-surfers and jet skis can be hired.

Suitability for tourists
1 The facilities allow tourists to spend a whole day there.
2 Many of the staff speak a second language.

Positive points
1 Good transport links to the city make the Club easily accessible.
2 Broad range of water sports would appeal to all kinds of people.
3 The area is very beautiful, and the sea is perfect for swimming.

Negative points
1 Prices in general are quite high.
2 The beach is not cleaned every day and so there is some rubbish near the tables.

Conclusion
In spite of the disadvantages, I would strongly recommend the Club for tourists.

---

7 Make a plan

Look at the notes for another tourist attraction. Make an outline for your report, using the following paragraph plan.

1 Introduction

2 General information

3 Facilities

4 Suitability for tourists

5 Positive points

6 Negative points

7 Conclusion

New National Archaeological Museum
- Entrance fee £1.50
- Right in the city centre
- Each period of history clearly divided into rooms
- Not open at weekends
- Cafeteria, shop, lift and access for wheelchairs
- Clear and well-presented displays
- Open Mon.-Fri., 9.30 a.m.-4.00 p.m.
- Commentary in variety of languages
- A lot to see in one day – can be tiring

8 Think about your introduction

a Look at the following introductions to a report asking you to assess the suitability of a new nightclub for foreign visitors. Decide which one is better and what is wrong with the other one.

1

> There are many good nightclubs in the city, and I believe that the best one is the Oasis, which opened last week.

2

> As requested, I have visited the new Oasis nightclub. The purpose of this report is to assess its suitability for foreign visitors to the town.

b Look at the outline you made in **7 Make a plan**. Write a suitable introduction to the report on the New National Archaeological Museum.

9 Think about your conclusion

a Look back at the model text on p.94 and decide what the purpose of the conclusion is.

b Look at the following conclusion for a report on a nightclub and decide if it is suitable.

> Finally I would like to say that I enjoyed visiting this nightclub very much. I'm sure you will agree with me if you go there yourself.

c Rewrite the conclusion in **b** so that it is appropriate for a report. (See **Writing Bank**, p.127.)

10 Think about grammar
Passives

a Look at the following sentences from the model text. Underline the verb forms that indicate a formal, impersonal style.

… and can be easily reached by public transport.

Wind-surfers and jet skis can be hired.

The beach is not cleaned every day, …

b Rewrite the following sentences in a more formal, impersonal style.

1 They don't keep the toilets clean.

....

2 They serve a different buffet lunch every day.

....

3 They don't clean the beach, so you can see rubbish everywhere.

....

4 They make all visitors feel welcome.

....

5 They provided tourist guides.

....

Exam practice: Write a report

You are going to write a report on the topic below. Do the tasks which follow.

> A group of foreign tourists is going to spend a holiday in your town. You have been asked to write a report for the group leader about eating out during their stay. Describe the best place for tourists to eat and drink in your area. Say what kind of food is available, and explain why you think this place would be suitable for tourists.

Write your **report** (120–180 words).

- **Read the question**
  Read the question and underline the key words.

- **Think about your reader**
  Identify your reader, and a suitable style for your answer.

- **Make a plan**
  Make an outline for your answer.

- **Think about format and style**
  Underline the headings for each main paragraph to make the report look clear. Number the details under each heading. Remember to use formal vocabulary in your report.

- **Think about grammar**
  Use passive verb forms to make your report impersonal.

- **Edit your text**
  Check your writing for errors when you have finished.

Further practice

Write a report on the topic below.

> You work for a company which organises cultural tours for foreign visitors. A group of tourists is coming for a holiday, and would like to visit a historical monument in your country. You have to write a report for your boss, describing a monument, saying why it would be interesting for foreign visitors, and recommending the best time of year to visit.

Write your **report** (120–180 words).

22 Evaluating proposals

1 Read the question

In Part 2 of the exam, you may be asked to write a report in which you evaluate proposals. **Read the exam question below and underline the key words.**

> Your town council has a large sum of money, which it is planning to spend on **either** a sports stadium **or** a theatre. You have been asked to write a report for the town council, describing the benefits of both projects and saying which one you think should be chosen, and why.

Write your **report** (120–180 words).

2 Think about your reader

Work with a partner. Look at the exam question again and answer the following questions.

1 What will your reader expect you to do? Choose the most complete answer.

  a say which plan you think is best

  b describe the advantages of both plans

  c describe the good points of both plans, recommend one and give reasons

  d describe the good points of both plans, and recommend one

  e describe the advantages and disadvantages of both plans, and recommend one

  f describe the disadvantages of both plans

2 Who do you think will read your report? Think about this person's job and how busy he/she might be.

3 Which style of writing will you use for your reader?

4 What format do you need to use?

tip

Remember that your reader will be a person in authority with a busy, sometimes stressful job. Your report should be written in such a way that:

- the reader can see at a glance the point of the report from your introduction and conclusion.
- the reader can quickly skim over the main headings and numbered details, to pick out important information in a hurry.
- the language is clear and concise with relatively short sentences.

3 Brainstorm the topic

a Work with a partner and answer the questions.

1 Look at the following list of facilities in a town or city and add some more examples.

- a theatre
- a sports stadium
- a museum
- a children's adventure park
- a swimming pool
- a library
- a recycling facility
- a zoo
- a skating rink
- a park for the blind

2 Which of the above facilities do you use? Why?

3 Which of the above facilities are most useful for the following people?

- teenagers
- very young children
- middle-aged people
- young couples
- the elderly
- college students
- unemployed people
- busy executives

4 Look at the photos and think of ways that the stadium and theatre might be used by a range of local people. Read the following comments and think of examples of your own.

- The coach of the local football team: 'A stadium would be a great place for holding national and international matches.'
- A middle-aged businessman: 'A theatre would allow me to see a great variety of shows and plays. At the moment, we have to travel to see decent live performances.'
- A young secretary: 'I'm an athletics fan. The stadium would mean I can see top-class competitions.'
- A keen amateur actor: 'There's nowhere really good to put on our Drama Society's performances – the theatre would be ideal for us.'
- An unemployed youth: 'A stadium might provide me with a job, as I'm interested in working in sports. There just aren't the jobs for people like me without this kind of facility.'
- A pensioner: 'I've always loved going to plays, and now I'm retired, a theatre would give me the perfect hobby.'

b Complete the table with notes from your discussion in **a**.

Benefits of a stadium	Benefits of a theatre

c After your discussion, would you choose the sports stadium or the theatre? Give reasons for your choice.

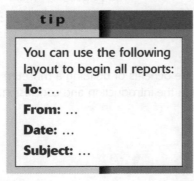

tip

You can use the following layout to begin all reports:

To: ...

From: ...

Date: ...

Subject: ...

22 Evaluating proposals

4 Read a model text

a Read the model text below, and write in the missing headings.

To: The Town Council
From: Charles Gregory
Date: 5 February 199-
Subject: Building project: Stadium or theatre?

_____

The purpose of this report is to recommend which building project would be most beneficial to the town.

_____

This would benefit the town in two main ways:

1 It would allow young people to participate in more sporting activities. The present facilities are inadequate and very old.

2 Professional competitions could be held, and people would be able to see top-class athletes, footballers and swimmers.

_____

This would offer the following advantages:

1 A variety of rock and classical concerts, operas and plays could be seen in the town, and it could even be used as a cinema.

2 It could be used to hold events for the local community, such as school concerts, and would be an ideal place for our local dance festival.

_____

While a theatre could offer many benefits, it would only appeal to a certain section of the population. In my opinion, the town council should build a sports stadium, because it could offer more facilities to a bigger range of people, both spectators and participants in sporting events. Furthermore, it would provide more job opportunities for the unemployed than the theatre would.

---

b Read the model text again and answer the following questions.

  1 Does the report contain all the points asked for in the exam question?

  2 Is the introduction suitable for the report?

  3 What is the purpose of the conclusion?

5 Think about paragraphing

a Look at the details under each heading in the model text and complete the outline below.

Paragraphs	Details
1 Introduction	
2	young people – more sport
3	concerts
4	

b Make an outline for a report on the benefits of building a museum or a children's adventure park in your town. Write the introduction and conclusion.

6 Think about vocabulary

a There are many expressions based on the verbs *make* or *do*. Look at the following example.

*This would **make a big difference** to our town, …*

b Complete the following sentences with the correct form of *make* or *do*.

1 The city can no longer .... without a good sports stadium.

2 We should all .... an effort to make this plan work.

3 There is still a lot of work to .... on the new underground train system.

4 We are trying to .... arrangements to meet the builders of the new theatre.

5 We hope to .... business with a French company.

6 Let's hope that the new stadium will .... money for the town.

7 The government is .... plans to build a new airport.

8 I hope that the town council will .... the right decision.

7 Think about grammar

Hypothetical situations

a The exam question on p.96 asks you to discuss plans for buildings which do not yet exist. When you discuss something hypothetically in this way, what verb form should you use? Look back at the model text on p.98, and underline examples of this form.

b Write two or three sentences, using the verb form in **a**, to discuss the advantages or disadvantages of the following plans for your town.

1 building a new motorway around your town

2 holding a three-day rock festival in the town's sports stadium

3 building cycle lanes along all roads, for the use of bicycles only

c Write a section of a report discussing the advantages and disadvantages of a plan to build an international airport near your town. Remember to use underlined headings, and to number the details in each paragraph.

Exam practice: Write a report

You are going to write a report on the topic below. Do the tasks which follow.

> Your local council is planning to build a new car park. There are two possible places for it: either on the site of a children's park, or next to a hospital. You have been asked to write a report to the town council, describing the advantages and disadvantages of each site and saying which one you would choose, and why.

Write your **report** (120–180 words).

- **Read the question**

  Read the question and underline the key words.

- **Think about your reader**

  Identify your reader, and a suitable style for your answer.

- **Make a plan**

  Make a list of advantages and disadvantages for each site. Decide which site you personally think is better. Choose the best ideas from your list, and make an outline for your report.

- **Think about paragraphing**

  Write an introduction stating the purpose of the report. Write clear headings for each paragraph and number the details. Write a conclusion, giving your opinion on the better site, with your reason(s).

- **Think about grammar**

  Remember to use *would* + infinitive to discuss hypothetical situations.

- **Edit your text**

  Check your writing for errors when you have finished.

Further practice

Write a report on the topic below.

> Your school has recently been given a large sum of money to spend on either a new library, or a cafeteria. You have been asked to write a report for your school director, describing the advantages of each plan. Say which one you think should be chosen, and why.

Write your **report** (120–180 words).

Reports

23 Suggesting improvements

1 Read the question

In Part 2 of the exam, you may be asked to write a report in which you make recommendations or suggest improvements. The contexts could be improvements to a library, museum, school, etc. **Read the exam question below and underline the key words.**

> You have a part-time job in a museum. The museum director wants to make the museum more popular with children aged 7–12. The director has asked you to write a report, making some recommendations.

Write your **report** (120–180 words).

2 Think about your reader

Work with a partner. Look at the exam question again and answer the following questions.

1 Who is going to read your report?

2 What will your reader expect you to do? Tick (✓) the correct option and say why the others would be inappropriate.
  a say why children find museums boring
  b suggest ways to attract more visitors to the museum
  c say what children like doing in museums
  d say why museums are only popular with tourists
  e suggest ways to make children want to visit the museum where you work

3 Brainstorm the topic

Work with a partner and answer the questions.

1 Look at the list of museums below. Tick (✓) the ones you have visited and add more examples to the list.
  • archaeological museum
  • history museum
  • natural history museum
  • science museum
  • waxworks museum

2 Make a list of what you can do at the museums in the above list, apart from looking at the exhibits.

3 Think of a visit to a museum and describe what you saw. Did you enjoy your visit? Why (not)?

4 Do you think it is a good idea for children to visit museums? Why?

5 Why do you think some museums are boring for young children?

6 What kind of things do children like doing? Add more ideas to the list.
  Children like:
  • drawing, painting and colouring
  • running and climbing
  • playing games

7 Look at the following ideas for making a museum more popular with children. Choose three or four ideas that you think would appeal to children most.

   a The museum could make leaflets of pictures of things in the museum. The children would have to find the things, and colour in the pictures in the correct colours.

   b The museum could make a leaflet, asking questions about things in the museum. The children would have to find the things and answer the questions. There could be a prize for the most complete answers.

   c There could be a taped description next to each thing on display in the museum. The children could press a button to hear the information.

   d There could be a room with copies of things in the museum that children could touch and play with.

   e There could be a fast-food cafeteria, so that children could rest, eat and drink.

   f The museum could have one day a week when only children could visit.

8 Add some more ideas to the list in **7**.

4 Edit your text

  a Read the following report and the teacher's comments. Rewrite the report to improve it in the ways suggested by the teacher.

To: The Museum Director
From: Ana García
Date: 23 August 199-
Subject: Recommendations to improve the popularity
              of the museum with children

Too informal. Write this in a more impersonal style.

Introduction

I'd like to report to you on the suggestions I've thought of to change the museum to get young children more interested.

Recommendations

Use a passive verb here.

1 We could give activity leaflets to children. The children would have to find the answers to questions by looking at the exhibits in the museum.

2 Pictures of the exhibits could be given to children, which could be coloured in according to what the exhibits look like.

Join this point to the previous one - it's part of the activity leaflet suggestion.

3 Another idea would be to have a room specially reserved for children. In the room would be copies of exhibits which the children could play with.

Make this passive.

4 The museum could employ someone as a guide, who knows how to stimulate children's interest. This could be a primary school teacher, or a mother who would like a part-time job.

5 The museum is far too boring for young children, as it doesn't offer anything for them to do.

Not relevant, as it's not a suggestion. Add another idea.

Add a heading to this section.

I believe that these suggestions would make the museum appeal to children and increase the number of school and family visits.

---

b Read the report in **a** on p.101 again, and answer the following questions.

1 Does the report contain all the points asked for in the exam question?

2 Does the report make relevant suggestions?

3 Is the report set out in the correct format?

4 Is there an appropriate conclusion?

5 Does the report have an acceptable number of words?

exam tip

Don't waste time in the exam counting the words you have written. You can calculate this roughly in the following way:

● Before the exam, work out the average number of words you write on one line.

● Count the number of lines you have written in your answer.

● Multiply the number of lines by the average number of words per line.

5 Think about vocabulary

Complete the following sentences with the correct form of the word in capitals.

1 The museum director is worried about the lack of .... of the museum. POPULAR

2 There is an interesting .... of Australian Aborigine art at the National Gallery. EXHIBIT

3 The new Science Museum has a large .... of fascinating displays. VARY

4 The site of ancient Delphi has always been a big tourist .... ATTRACT

5 I think that all children are interested in .... facts. SCIENCE

6 In my opinion, we need someone who has a good .... of children. UNDERSTAND

7 Children love learning, due to their natural .... CURIOUS

8 We should try to stimulate children's .... CREATIVE

6 Think about style

a Look at the following examples from the report in **4 Edit your text a**. Underline the verb forms which make the suggestions more formal and polite.

Pictures of the exhibits could be given to children ...

In the room would be copies of exhibits which the children could play with.

Another idea would be to have a room ...

b Write two suggestions in a formal style for each of the following questions.

1 Can you suggest how to make a bookshop more popular with children?

2 Can you suggest how to improve the place where you work or study?

3 Can you suggest how to improve a local park to make it safer for children?

4 Can you suggest how to improve the roads to make them safer for pedestrians?

Exam practice: Write a report

You are going to write a report on the topic below. Do the tasks which follow.

The school where you study English is considering making improvements to the classrooms. You have been asked to write a report for your head teacher, making suggestions on how the classrooms can be improved.

Write your **report** (120–180 words).

- **Read the question**

  Read the question and underline the key words.

- **Think about your reader**

  Identify your reader, and a suitable style for your answer.

- **Brainstorm the topic**

  Think about the classroom where you study English. What are its good and bad points? What would you like to see in your classroom? What new equipment would you like your classroom to have? What could be done to decorate the classroom?

- **Make a plan**

  Make an outline for your report. Make sure you deal with one main idea in each paragraph.

- **Think about style**

  Make sure you use the correct verb forms to write polite suggestions in an impersonal way.

- **Edit your text**

  Check your writing for errors when you have finished.

Further practice

Write a report on the topic below.

You work part time in a library. The manager wants to make the library more popular with teenagers, and has asked you to write a report making some recommendations.

Write your **report** (120–180 words).

24 Describing people and relationships

1 Read the question

In Part 2 of the exam, you may be asked to write an article for a magazine, a newspaper or a book. **Read the exam question below and underline the key words.**

> A publishing company plans to publish a book called *People to Remember*. The book will include short articles about politicians, writers, musicians, sports personalities and other people who have been important in your country in some way. You have been invited to write a short article for this book, describing a person and saying why he/she is/was important in your country.

Write your **article** (120–180 words).

exam tip

In Part 2 of the exam, the articles can be on different topics and in different styles. You can write in a serious, humorous, formal or informal style, depending on who is going to read your article.

2 Think about your reader

Work with a partner. Look at the exam question again and answer the following questions. (Sometimes more than one answer is possible.)

1 Who would your reader expect you to write about?

a a politician, writer, musician or sports personality who has influenced your country

b a person who is important in your town

c someone who has influenced you personally

d any important person who has had an effect on your country

tip

When you are writing an article, imagine a specific kind of reader to help you write in an appropriate style, e.g. a teenage student, a historian, an adult needing something to read on holiday, etc.

2 What would your reader expect to find in your article?

- Tick (✓) all the options which could apply to your article.
- Which options should be the main part of your article?
- Which options can be mentioned briefly as background?
- Which options are not relevant?

a details of the person's childhood

b anecdotes about the person

c information about the person's personal likes and dislikes

d when and where the person was born

e a description of the person's physical appearance

f an account of the person's achievements

g reasons why the person is important

h a short history of your country

3 Brainstorm the topic

Work with a partner and answer the questions.

1 What kind of people do you think are important? Add more examples to the following list.

- politicians
- writers
- musicians
- sports personalities
- film stars

2 Think of some people who have been important in your country. Say why they are important, using the following questions to help you.

  a Have they done something that you admire?

  b Have they been very successful in their career?

  c Have they made other people's lives better in some way?

  d Have they done something to help your country?

  e Are they people you would like to be yourself? Why?

  f Have they done something very dangerous, or very courageous?

  g Have they managed to cope well with a difficult problem?

3 Think of some more reasons why someone might be important in a country.

4 Which person would you like to write about in your answer to the exam question?

4 Read a model text

a Read the model text and answer the questions below.

One name that sports fans will always remember is Earvin Johnson Jnr, known to the public as 'Magic' Johnson. His early success in basketball saw him winning championships in school and university. He then went on to become the captain of the Lakers team, and was a star in the 1992 Olympic Games.

Some players are good because they have one particular skill, but 'Magic' Johnson was great as he had remarkable talent in all areas of the game. Due to his everlasting smile and endless energy, he was also an inspiring team leader. He always believed in himself and in his team, and would do anything to win the game.

Outside the world of basketball, he is also important because of his role in business. Since he believes that every enterprise should be of value to society, his companies have brought employment to poverty-stricken inner cities. In addition, he has been involved in many charities, using his fame to benefit the underprivileged.

I believe that 'Magic' Johnson has brought opportunity and happiness not only to basketball fans, but also to young people needing a chance to succeed in life.

1 Does the article contain all the points asked for in the exam question?

2 Is the content of the article suitable for inclusion in the book *People to Remember*?

3 Is the article written in an appropriate style?

b Write a brief summary of each paragraph in the model text on p.105 in the spaces below.

```
 ( 1 ) → ( 2 ) → ( 3 ) → ( 4 )
```

5 Make a plan

Make a plan for an article about Mother Teresa, using the notes below. Organise the notes into an outline like the one in **4 Read a model text b**, using the following questions to help you.

1 What background information can go into the introduction?

2 What will you include in the main paragraphs?

3 What information would be suitable for the conclusion?

> _Mother Teresa of Calcutta_
> Born 1910, in Albania
> Nun from age 18, went to India
> Famous for helping the poor in India
> Saw sick and dying people on Calcutta streets
> Started the order 'Missionaries of Charity' to
>   help in India, then all over the world
> Completely unselfish
> Gave her life to the poor, sick and hungry
> Had no money or personal possessions
> Nobel Peace Prize, 1979
> Died 1997, thousands cried when she died, many
>   world figures (e.g. Queen of Spain, Hillary
>   Clinton, President of Italy) at her funeral

6 Think about vocabulary

a Complete the following sentences, using the words and phrases in the box.
Make any necessary changes.

1 Sir Isaac Newton greatly .... our understanding of physics today.

2 I have tremendous .... for the way that Mother Teresa helped the poor.

3 Salvador Dali was one of the most .... artists of the 20th century.

4 Henry Ford .... his .... to make a cheap car that everyone could afford.

5 Sir Alexander Fleming made one of the greatest .... in medicine, penicillin, almost by accident.

6 Thomas Edison is well known as the .... of the electric light.

7 Mother Teresa .... her whole life to helping the poor.

8 Alexander the Great .... the city of Alexandria in Egypt.

9 Marie Curie was a .... in the field of research into radioactivity.

admiration

creative

devote

discovery

found

influence

inventor

pioneer

realise an ambition

b Complete the table with the correct form of the words.

Noun	Verb	Adjective	Person
	influence		X
admiration			
		creative	
ambition	X		X
achievement		X	
	devote		X
			inventor
	discover	X	

7 Think about connectors

a Look at the following sentences from the model text. Underline the words or phrases which introduce a reason.

Some players are good because they have one particular skill, …

… 'Magic' Johnson was great as he had remarkable talent in all areas of the game.

Due to his everlasting smile and endless energy, he was also …

Since he believes that every enterprise should be of value to society, his companies …

b Write five sentences about people you like and/or admire, giving suitable reasons. Use a different word or phrase to introduce the reason in each sentence.

Exam practice: Write an article

You are going to write an article on the topic below. Do the tasks which follow.

You have seen this advertisement in a magazine.

> **C O M P E T I T I O N**
>
> *Write and tell us what you think makes a good friend. The winning article will be published in our international magazine, Now!, and the winner will receive a prize of £500.*

Write your **article** (120–180 words).

- **Read the question**

  Read the question and underline the key words.

- **Think about your reader**

  Identify your reader, and a suitable style for your answer.

- **Brainstorm the topic**

  Think about your best friend. Write down all the reasons why he/she is your best friend. Think about his/her character and the things he/she does. Write down examples of important or special things he/she has done, and of memorable experiences you have had together. Write down the three most important qualities a good friend should have.

- **Make a plan**

  Make an outline for your article, grouping your notes into clear paragraphs.

- **Think about paragraphing**

  Include the three most important qualities of your friend in the introduction. Take one quality for your first paragraph, and write a topic sentence. Then add supporting details. You could tell small anecdotes from your experience, or give reasons. Follow the same format for the other main paragraphs. Write a conclusion to summarise the idea of friendship, saying, for example, that good friends are hard to find, or that good friendships last a long time.

- **Edit your text**

  Check your writing for errors when you have finished.

Further practice

Write an article on the topic below.

> Your college magazine has invited you to write an article with the title:
> *The person who has had the greatest influence on my life.*

Write your **article** (120–180 words).

25 Reviewing

1 Read the question

In Part 2 of the exam, you may be asked to write a review on something you have seen, heard, read or experienced. **Read the exam question below and underline the key words.**

You have seen this advertisement in a newspaper:

> ## *International Students' Magazine*
>
> We are looking for articles on favourite TV programmes around the world. Write an article, answering these questions:
>
> • What's your favourite programme?
> • Why do you like it?
>
> The best articles will be published in next month's magazine.

Write your **article** for *International Students' Magazine* (120–180 words).

2 Think about your reader

Work with a partner. Look at the exam question again and answer the following questions.

1 What is the name of the magazine which will publish your article?

2 Who do you think buys this magazine?

3 Which style of writing will you use for your reader?

   a very chatty and colloquial

   b formal and impersonal

   c relatively informal with a personal tone

4 Do you think the reader will know the programme you are reviewing?

5 What basic information should you give at the beginning of your article?

> **tip**
>
> A review is a type of article in which you usually have to give your opinion, and often make recommendations. The review may be of a TV programme, a film, a play, a place you have visited, etc.

3 Think about vocabulary

a Work with a partner. Make a list of all the types of programmes that you can see on TV.

b Look at the following extract from a TV guide and underline all the types of programme.

6.00	Party of Five — American sitcom
6.50	Fresh Pop — all the latest from this fast-moving music show
7.00	News and Weather
7.55	Mind Olympics — quiz show with a difference
8.00	Brookside — the latest happenings in Liverpool's favourite soap
8.30	The Hanging Gale — more in the dramatic serial from Ireland
9.00	Black Box — what happens when pilots make errors of judgement. Documentary
10.00	Ally McBeal — legal drama series
11.00	Film: The Diviners (1992)
1.30	The World Tonight — current affairs programme
2.00	Steptoe and Son — classic comedy series
2.30	The Jonathon Ross Show — chat show

c The words in the box below are often used to describe books, films and TV programmes. Complete the table with words of similar meaning from the box.

good	bad	funny	interesting	boring	exciting

amusing   appalling   awful   brilliant   dramatic   dreadful
dreary   dull   excellent   fascinating   fast-paced   gripping   hilarious
humorous   outstanding   superb   tedious   thrilling   witty

d Add more examples to each category in the table in **c**.

exam tip

Try to use a broad range of vocabulary in the exam. For example, if you are asked to describe someone or something, avoid repeating simple adjectives like *good, bad, funny,* etc. and use more sophisticated words like *brilliant, awful, hilarious,* etc.

4 Brainstorm the topic

Work with a partner and answer the questions.

1 What kind of programmes appeal to you most?

2 Which programme is your favourite? Why?

3 Describe your favourite programme, using the following questions to help you.

a What kind of programme is it?

b Who are the people in it?

c What is the purpose of the programme?

d If the programme tells a story, what is the setting? Who are the main characters? What happens?

e If it is another kind of programme, what is it about? Is there a regular cast, or do you see different people each time?

f What other aspects of the programme do you like? Think about theme music, the script, the cast, the quality of acting or presenting, etc.

g What kind of people does the programme mainly appeal to? Why would you recommend it to them?

h If you had to choose three adjectives to describe your favourite programme, which words would you choose?

5 Read a model text

a Read the model text and answer the following questions.

1 What background information does the writer give the reader in the introduction?

2 What is the purpose of the writer's conclusion?

3 What tense does the writer use to review the programme?

My favourite TV programme is 'Friends'. It's a brilliantly funny American sitcom about a group of friends who live in New York. Each character has a distinct personality, and they are always getting into strange, sad or hilarious situations.

This show is one of my favourites because the characters are so strongly portrayed. My favourites are Chandler and Phoebe. Chandler is unlucky in love, because he always seems to choose the wrong sort of girl. Phoebe is an eccentric who always has something strange or irrelevant to say, but all her friends accept her for who she is.

Another reason I love this programme is that the script is so witty that I laugh from beginning to end. There aren't many other programmes that leave me helpless with laughter throughout!

I suppose the main reason why this show appeals to me so much is that it reflects our own lives, but in an amusing way, so that we can laugh at our own problems. This is one of the funniest shows I have ever seen, and you should not miss it if you can see it where you live!

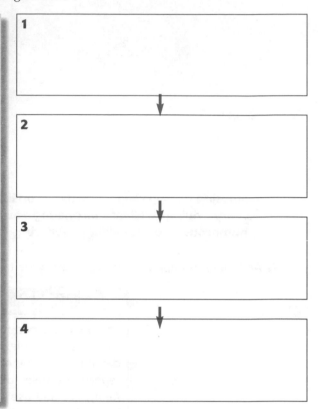

b Underline the topic sentences in the model text. Then complete the outline of the model text by making notes in the boxes.

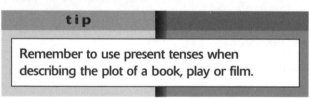

tip

Remember to use present tenses when describing the plot of a book, play or film.

6 Make a plan

a Make an outline for your own favourite TV programme like the one above. Make notes on relevant aspects from the following list.

- the script
- the plot
- the actors/acting
- the production
- the scenes
- the characters

b Write an introduction for your article, giving the background information to your reader.

c Write a conclusion for your article, with a summary and a recommendation to your reader.

7 **Think about grammar**

Superlatives and the Present Perfect

a Look at the following example from the model text. Underline the adjective, and the following verb form.

This is one of the funniest shows I have ever seen, …

b Write a true sentence following the pattern in **a** and using the following words.

e.g. *frightening film – Alien is one of the most frightening films I have ever seen.*

1 awful trip	**5** inspiring person
2 hilarious programme	**6** gripping book
3 fascinating person	**7** entertaining game
4 thrilling experience	**8** dreadful concert

Exam practice: Write an article

You are going to write an article on the topic below. Do the tasks which follow.

> Your favourite magazine is organising a writing competition this month. The prize is a three-day weekend in London, with a visit to a film studio. Write an article, describing a film that you have enjoyed, and explaining why you would recommend it to others.

Write your **article** (120–180 words).

- **Read the question**

  Read the question and underline the key words.

- **Think about your reader**

  Think about who reads the magazine and who will read your article.

- **Think about vocabulary**

  Think of two or three adjectives that give the overall impression of the film.
  You can use these in your introduction, and/or in the conclusion.

- **Make a plan**

  Make an outline of the main points for each paragraph, including relevant recommendations.

- **Think about your conclusion**

  Summarise your opinions, remembering to include your final recommendation.

- **Edit your text**

  Check your writing for errors when you have finished.

Further practice

Write an article on the topic below.

You have seen this announcement on the noticeboard in your school:

> **School magazine:** **To all students**
>
> Next month we would like to publish articles about the best concert you have been to, and why it was so special. We hope that a lot of students will contribute.
>
> Please hand in all articles by the end of this month.

Write your **article** for the magazine (120–180 words).

26 Language learning

1 Read the question

The subject of language learning often comes up in Part 2 of the exam. You may be asked to write letters and reports, but also articles about your experience of learning a language. **Read the exam question below and underline the key words.**

> Your college magazine has invited you to suggest helpful ways of improving your speaking ability in English. Write an article for the magazine, giving your suggestions, and referring to your experience.

Write your **article** (120–180 words).

2 Think about your reader

Work with a partner. Look at the exam question again and answer the following questions.

1 What kind of magazine will your article be published in?

2 How old are the readers?

3 What will your reader expect you to do?

  a write a story about your experiences of learning English

  b make some suggestions about improving speaking, giving examples from your own experience

  c write a list of suggestions about improving speaking

  d make some suggestions about the best way to learn English

> **tip**
>
> Always remember to read the question carefully. Find the main topics and underline the key words before you start to write.

3 Brainstorm the topic

Work with a partner and answer the questions.

1 How do you feel about speaking in English?

2 Where do you speak English? Who do you speak to?

3 What are your main problems in speaking?

4 What do you do to practise speaking? Think about your time in class and outside the classroom.

5 In your country, do you have TV programmes, radio stations or films in English? Do they help you to improve your spoken English?

6 Make a list of suggestions to help someone improve their spoken English.

> **tip**
>
> Always spend a few minutes brainstorming the question, and use your experience or knowledge about the topic to help you come up with ideas.

4 Think about style

Read the three extracts below from answers to the exam question. Which one is written in the most appropriate style? Why are the other two not suitable?

1
> The essential ingredient in speaking a foreign language is practice. Students should be encouraged to avail themselves of every opportunity to speak that presents itself, both inside and outside the classroom.

2
> One of the most entertaining ways to improve your speaking is to learn the words of your favourite songs. Sing along whenever you hear them, and you will get a feel for the rhythm of the language.

3
> • Try to talk to native speakers of English.
> • Watch TV programmes in English.
> • Don't be afraid of making mistakes.
> • Don't speak your own language in lessons.

5 Read a model text

a Read the model text and tick (✓) which of the topics in the list below are included in the article.

1 the problems of speaking in a foreign language
2 suggestions for getting speaking practice in class
3 suggestions for getting speaking practice outside class
4 how your teacher can help you
5 the kind of attitude that will help to improve speaking
6 how reading and listening can help
7 the best way to improve speaking
8 things which do not help to improve speaking

> **tip**
>
> When you write an article, you can add a title, like a newspaper headline.

Lost for words?

Have you been studying English for years, but still can't say a word? Do you suddenly lose confidence when you have to speak to someone? I had the same problems, but I've managed to find ways to overcome them.

First of all, adopting a positive attitude is essential. You should never be afraid of making a mistake or worry that people will laugh at you. Only then can you really start to speak. Most people listen for the meaning of what you are trying to say, and do not notice your mistakes.

Secondly, you should try to get as much speaking practice as possible. In class, answer as many questions as possible, and try to participate in class discussions. When you are on holiday, try to make contact with other English-speakers, and who knows? You might make some good friends in this way.

My problem has always been vocabulary. I find that watching TV programmes in English and reading increase my exposure to new words, and help me recycle words I know in new contexts.

I hope that you will find my suggestions useful. Don't waste any more time! Get speaking English now!

b Read the model text again and find the parts of the article where the writer mentions his/her own experience. What problems does the writer mention?

c Underline the topic sentences for paragraphs 2, 3 and 4.

d Write a brief summary of each paragraph in the spaces below.

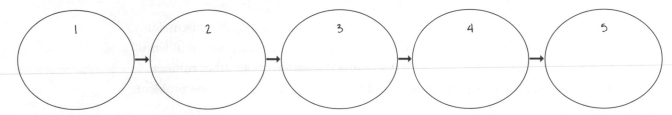

6 Think about your introduction

Look back at the introduction to the model text. How does the writer get the reader's attention? Write introductions in the same way for the following topics.

> **tip**
>
> In articles of this type, it's important to get the reader's attention. One way of doing this is to 'talk' directly to the reader, by asking questions, giving direct advice, etc.

1 an article about ways to remember new vocabulary
2 an article to suggest ways to improve listening skills
3 an article about the best ways to study a foreign language

26 Language learning

7 Make a plan

a Look back at the notes you made for **3 Brainstorm the topic 6**. Choose three of your best ideas and decide which ideas belong in each paragraph.

b Write a topic sentence for each paragraph.

c Write an introduction and conclusion for your article.

8 Think about vocabulary

a Look at the following examples which were used in the model text on p.113. Underline the verbs.

overcome a problem   *participate in a discussion*
lose confidence   *waste time*

b What other verbs can be used with the nouns in **a**?

c Form sets of words that go together like the examples in **a**. Complete the table,

a problem	confidence	a discussion	time
overcome	lose	participate in	waste

build up   come up against   cut short   destroy   encounter   gain   get into
get involved in   have   run into   run out of   save   shatter   solve   spend

using the words and phrases in the box.

d Look back at the table in **c**. Which two examples from the box can go in two different columns? Which example can go in every column?

e Complete the following sentences with the correct form of the expressions in the table in **c**. (Sometimes more than one answer is possible.)

1 This traffic is terrible. You'll .... time by going on foot.

2 While trying to connect my computer, I .... a problem.

3 A good teacher can really .... your confidence.

4 I didn't finish the exam, because I .... time.

5 We started to argue, so I decided to .... the discussion.

6 When I fell off my bike, it completely .... my confidence.

7 We .... an interesting discussion about other cultures.

8 After several hours, we finally managed to .... the problem.

9 Think about grammar

Inversion for emphasis

a Look at the following sentence from the model text on p.113. What word order is used after *Only then*? Where would you normally find this kind of word order?

Only then can you really start to speak.

Showing emphasis

When you want to give a point extra emphasis, you can use inversion. Start the sentence with *Only then* and write the verb form as if it were a question, e.g.

We took every opportunity to practise. We started to see results.

We took every opportunity to practise. Only then did we start to see results.

b Rewrite the second sentence in the following examples, starting with *Only then*.

1 I read a lot in English. I made faster progress then.

....

2 The teacher corrected my mistake. I didn't understand what was wrong until this moment.

....

3 You have to be confident. You will speak more fluently then.

....

4 You must get a lot of practice. Then you should take the examination.

....

5 She decided not to worry about mistakes. At that moment her confidence grew.

....

> **tip**
>
> **You can use inversion for emphasis, or to be dramatic in a narrative, but don't use this technique too often!**

Exam practice: Write an article

You are going to write an article on the topic below. Do the tasks which follow.

> An international students' magazine is asking for students around the world to write articles about their language-learning experiences. The article should answer the question:
> *What is the best way to learn a foreign language?*
> Write an article for the magazine, describing your experiences, and suggesting the best way to learn a language.

Write your **article** (120–180 words).

- **Read the question**

  Read the question and underline the key words.

- **Think about your reader**

  Identify your reader, and a suitable style for your answer.

- **Brainstorm the topic**

  Brainstorm a list of ideas for your article. Think about the answers to the following questions:

  1 Is it better to study alone, or in a class?

  2 Is it better to study in an English-speaking country, or in your own country?

  3 What is the best way to learn grammar, vocabulary, writing, etc?

  4 What ways to learn a language have you tried that have been successful?

- **Make a plan**

  Choose three or four of the best ideas, and make an outline of your article, adding some details for each paragraph. Make notes of examples from your own experience.

- **Think about your introduction**

  In the introduction, ask the readers questions to get their attention.

- **Link your text**

  Write a topic sentence for each paragraph, where necessary. Use sequencing words and phrases to show the order of your ideas, e.g. *In the first place …, Secondly …,* etc.

- **Edit your text**

  Check your writing for errors when you have finished.

Further practice

Write an article on the topic below.

You have seen this advertisement in an English student magazine:

> **C O M P E T I T I O N**
>
> *Write and tell us what your main problems are in learning English, and the ways you have tried to overcome them. The best articles will be published in next month's issue, and the winners will receive six books of their choice.*

Write your **article** (120–180 words).

27 Discussing the plot

1 Optional set book questions

In question 5 of Part 2 of the exam, you may choose to answer **one** question from a choice of two on a set book. The questions on set books are often about the plot, or the characters in the book. The answers you are asked to write are usually compositions, but sometimes you will be asked to write a letter, an article, a story or a report.

> **tip**
>
> As you read your chosen book, you should underline main events in the story. Keep a notebook and make notes on the main events in each chapter as you read. When you have finished reading, you will have a complete synopsis of the story.

2 Make notes on the plot

Look at the following 'notes' on the story *William Wilson* in *Tales of Mystery and Imagination*. They are too long and detailed for a summary and are written like a composition. Summarise the most important events and facts in note form, using the following headings to help you.

- background to story/early years
- his first school
- Eton
- university/the card game
- travels/Rome

William Wilson is not the narrator's real name, but he is too ashamed to tell us his real identity because he has led an evil life. He tells us that he is writing his story so that he can feel less guilty about all his wrong-doings. He tells us that he was always a person with a violent temper, and this worried his family. He was always allowed to have his own way in everything that he did. He describes his schooldays where he became the leader of his friends. There was one boy (also called William Wilson) who refused to follow him, and who always copied his schoolwork, his way of dressing and his voice. This boy also gave William advice as often as he could. William became furious and made fun of this boy to try and defeat him. William later went to Eton, another school, and was a very lazy, unpleasant student who drank heavily. One night he had a strange visitor who simply said his name, shook his finger in warning, and then disappeared. William thought it was the boy, the other William Wilson, from his first school. When William went to university, he began to enjoy cheating at cards. One night, while playing cards with a man called Glendinning, he cheated again, and took all Glendinning's money. This young man was totally ruined, and became very white in the face. Suddenly the lights went out, and a voice told the company that William had cheated. William believed that it was the other Wilson. William had to leave the university in shame. He travelled to many places, but he was always followed by the other Wilson, who interrupted his life in many ways. Finally, in Rome, he fought with the other Wilson, and killed him. He realised as the other Wilson was dying that he was in fact himself, and that by killing him, he had killed himself.

Making notes

When making notes, you should:

- select only the key events, and leave out the more detailed parts of the story.
- miss out words like articles, auxiliary verbs, connectors, etc.
- use headings and numbers to organise your notes.
- use abbreviations.

3 Read the question

Read the exam question below and underline the key words.

> Answer the following question based on your reading of **one** of the set books.
> Your answer should contain enough detail to make it clear to someone who may
> not have read the book.
> Which part of the book do you think is the most important?

Write a **composition** briefly describing the part you have chosen, and explaining
your reasons for choosing it (120–180 words).

4 Think about your reader

Work with a partner. Look at the exam question again and answer the following questions.

1 What will your reader expect you to do? Choose the best answer from the
   list below:
   a write a summary of the plot of the book
   b write a summary of one of the chapters and say why it is important
   c write a summary of part of the book which is important to you and
     say why
   d describe an event in the book which has affected you in some way

2 What form should your answer take?
   a a story
   b a composition
   c an article
   d a report

3 Does the exam question specify who the reader will be?

4 Which style of writing will you use for your reader?

---

exam tip

- If you are asked to write a composition and
  the reader is not specified, write it as if it
  were for your teacher.
- When you write, imagine that the reader
  has not read the story.

---

5 Brainstorm the topic

Work with a partner and answer the questions.

1 Think about the set book of your choice. What do you think is the most
   important part of the book? Describe what happened in this part.

2 Why is the part you have chosen the most important? Choose from the following
   reasons, or give another reason of your own.
   a This part of the book solved a mystery.
   b In this part of the book, I found out something surprising.
   c Something dramatic happened.
   d Something sad or tragic happened.
   e Something happy or good happened.
   f This was a very exciting part of the book.

6 Read a model text

a Look at the paragraph beginnings and extracts from a model text on *The Old Man and the Sea*. Which beginning goes with which extract?

a The part of the book I think is most important is …	**c** Finally, …
b The event takes place …	**d** I think this is an important part of the book because …

1 … on the third day, Santiago manages to kill the fish with a harpoon, and because it is too big to put on the boat, he ties it to the side. It is his greatest triumph, but sadly, sharks eat the fish before he arrives home.

2 … when Santiago finally catches the big fish. I think anyone who reads this story will agree that this is the climax of the book.

3 … it shows how an old man can battle against nature, and win. Santiago suffers a lot, but shows great determination and courage struggling against both the marlin and the sharks. Although he loses the marlin, he gains the status of a hero.

4 … after Santiago has spent 84 days without catching a fish. When he sails far out to sea one day, he manages to catch a marlin on his hook, but the fish is enormous, and he spends two days struggling to land it. He becomes very tired and injured in the process.

b Complete the following outline for your answer on the set book you have chosen.

Paragraph	First sentence	Details
1 Introduction State which part of the book is the most important		
2 Main paragraph Describe the event(s) briefly		
3 Main paragraph What finally happened		
4 Conclusion Reason why you think it is important		

c Write your composition, using the model in **a** and outline in **b** to help you.

7 Think about vocabulary

Complete the following sentences, using the correct form of the words in the box.

The Old Man and the Sea

1 The .... is very simple, and takes place mainly over three days.

2 The book is .... off the coast of Cuba, probably in the 1940s.

3 The .... of the story is a man called Santiago.

4 The story is about an old man, a boy and the sea, with very few ....

Wuthering Heights

5 Hindley Earnshaw is the .... of the story; he is evil and cruel in the way he treats Heathcliff.

6 The .... of this story is Catherine Earnshaw.

7 Emily Brontë .... Linton Heathcliff as spoiled and selfish.

8 The plot .... through the narrative of Mrs Dean, as told to Mr Lockwood.

develop   hero   heroine   minor character   plot   portray   set   villain

8 Think about tenses

Look at following extract from a summary of the plot of *Wuthering Heights*.
Complete the extract with the correct form of the verb in brackets.

Mr Lockwood, the narrator of the story, (1) .... (rent) a house
called Thrushcross Grange on the Yorkshire moors. He (2) ....
(visit) his landlord, Mr Heathcliff, and (3) .... (stay) in his house,
Wuthering Heights, where he (4) .... (have) a strange dream
about a woman called Catherine Linton. When he (5) .... (return)
home, he (6) .... (ask) his housekeeper, Mrs Dean, about
Catherine and Wuthering Heights. Mrs Dean then (7) .... (tell)
him the story of the Earnshaws, their children Hindley and Cathy, and
Heathcliff, a gypsy boy adopted by Mr Earnshaw. Hindley is cruel to
Heathcliff, but Cathy (8) .... (fall) in love with him. Cathy later
(9) .... (go) to stay with their neighbours, the Lintons, at their
house which is called Thrushcross Grange. She (10) .... (come)
home a changed person, and later (11) .... (marry) Edgar Linton.
Heathcliff is so upset that he (12) .... (run) away and is not
heard of for many years.

Exam practice: Write a composition

You are going to write a composition on the topic below. Do the tasks which follow.

> Think about the ending of the book or story you have read. Were you satisfied with it?

Write a **composition**, describing the ending and explaining how you felt about it
(120–180 words).

- **Read the question**

  Read the question and underline the key words. Remember that the question tells you to
  write a composition (not a letter, story, etc.).

- **Think about your reader**

  Identify your reader, and a suitable style for your answer.

- **Make a plan**

  Make an outline for your composition as follows:

  1 Introduction – say whether your story has a happy, sad or mysterious ending.

  2 Main paragraph – briefly describe what happens at the end of the book.

  3 Conclusion – write your opinion of the ending, giving reasons.

- **Think about tenses**

  Use present tenses to write about the events in a book or story.

- **Edit your text**

  Check your writing for errors when you have finished.

Further practice

Write a composition on the topic below.

> You and your fellow students would like to make a video of one part of the book you
> have read. Describe the part of the book you would most like to film, and give reasons
> why it would make a good video.

Write your **composition** (120–180 words).

28 Discussing characters

1 Optional set book questions

In question 5 of Part 2 of the exam, you may be asked to write about the characters in the
book you have read. This could be about the main characters, or the minor characters.

2 Makes notes on the text

> **tip**
>
> While you are reading the book of your choice, use a section of your notebook
> to make notes on characters. Use one page for each main character in the
> book. As you read each chapter, make notes under the headings *Appearance,
> Style of dress, Personal habits, Personality – good points and bad points,* etc.
> Add examples or quotations from the book under each heading to support the
> comments you make about characters in the exam.

Look at the notes below on the character of Catherine Earnshaw, the heroine of
Wuthering Heights. Make similar notes about one of the characters from a set book or
story of your choice.

<u>Catherine Earnshaw</u>
<u>Personality</u>   <u>Examples from the story</u>

- wild and headstrong   • runs wild with Heathcliff on
                                                 moors
                                             • loses shoe, races with
                                                 Heathcliff barefoot

- contrast – ladylike behaviour • returns from Lintons with
                                                 smart clothes, worries about
                                                 getting dirty
                                             • agrees to marry Edgar

- bad-tempered   • hits Mrs Dean, Hareton and
                                                 Edgar

> **tip**
>
> Do not simply describe a character. You must
> support your description with examples of
> the character's actions in the story, and/or
> add quotations.

3 Read the question

Read the exam question below and underline the key words.

> Write a short article for your college magazine about the character in a book you
> would most like to meet. Describe the character, and say why you would like to
> meet him/her.

Write your **article** (120–180 words).

4 Think about your reader

Work with a partner. Look at the exam question again and answer the following questions.

1 What will your reader expect you to do?

    a write a story describing what your favourite character does in the book, and why you like him/her

    b write a composition describing the character you most dislike

    c write a description of the character you would most like to talk to, and what you would say if you could meet

    d write an article describing the character you would like to get to know, and why you would like to meet him/her

2 Who is going to read your article?

3 Which style of writing will you use for your reader?

    a very informal and chatty

    b formal and academic

    c fairly informal and personal

    d formal and very impersonal

5 Brainstorm the topic

Work with a partner and answer the questions.

1 Write down the names of the main and minor characters in the book or story of your choice. For each one, discuss the following points.

    ● character's role (hero/heroine/villain, etc.)

    ● appearance

    ● personality

    ● actions that illustrate personality

    ● least likeable character

    ● most likeable character

    ● most interesting character

    ● strangest character

2 Which character would you most like to meet? Why?

3 If you met this character, what questions would you like to ask him/her?

6 Think about content

a Read the following extracts from *The Old Man and the Sea, Wuthering Heights* and *Tales of Mystery and Imagination*. Say if the extracts mainly describe:

    1 the person's attitudes and opinions

    2 the person's character and behaviour

1 Usher, *Tales of Mystery and Imagination*

'He suffered a great deal from a sharpness of the senses. He could eat only tasteless food, and wear only a certain kind of clothing. He could not bear the smell of flowers. The faintest light brought pain to his eyes; and he had forbidden all sounds in the house, except those from certain musical instruments.'

2 Santiago, *The Old Man and the Sea*

'He was very fond of flying fish as they were his principal friends on the ocean. He was sorry for the birds, especially the small delicate dark terns that were always flying and looking and almost never finding, and he thought, "The birds have a harder life than we do except for the robber birds and the heavy strong ones."

3 Santiago, *The Old Man and the Sea*

'He took all his pain and what was left of his strength and his long-gone pride and he put it against the fish's agony and the fish came over onto his side, ...'

4 Catherine, *Wuthering Heights*

Her spirits were always high, her tongue was always going — singing, laughing, interrupting everybody. She was a wild, wicked young thing, but she had the prettiest eye and sweetest smile and lightest foot in our part of the country, and after all, I think she meant no harm.'

5 Heathcliff, *Wuthering Heights*

'His walk lacked confidence, he looked unpleasant and rarely spoke, and he took pleasure in stirring up the dislike of those whom he met.'

b Choose the best words and phrases from the box to refer to Usher, Santiago, Catherine or Heathcliff, as described in the extracts in **a**. Not all the words and phrases are used.

anti-social	attractive	bad-tempered	depressed	determined	generous
high-spirited	honest	loving	over-sensitive	respectful of nature	ridiculous

> **exam tip**
>
> If you are asked to write about a character in the exam, make sure you mainly give details about their personality and behaviour. Only refer to their appearance if this is relevant to the question.

7 Be your own examiner

Read the model text and use the checklists in the table on p.123 to evaluate its strengths and weaknesses. Do not focus on the underlined words at this stage.

> I would like to meet Heathcliff in 'Wuthering Heights'. Sometimes we hate him, and other times we feel sorry for him. Catherine seems to both like him and hate him too, as she is a very difficult person, with unpredictable emotions.
>
> He is very passionate, and feels things more underline{deep} than normal people. He wants revenge for all the bad things that have happened to him, and he does bad things to show how deeply he loves Catherine. He often wants to behave better, and tries to change in his younger days. Catherine loves him, but the snobbish side of her character rejects him, and she marries someone else.
>
> He thinks he hasn't done underline{nothing} wrong, and he doesn't feel guilty for all the bad things he has done. He becomes rich and well-educated, and he treats the other people in the story badly. He is very independent and intelligent, and life has been hard for him and his personality has been changed underline{from} all the bad things that people have done to him in the past. He wants revenge on Catherine for marrying Edgar, and on Hindley for treating him badly as a child.
>
> I would like to meet him and I would like to ask him many questions and I think we underline{had} a very interesting conversation if we could meet.

Content	Style and format
• Is there a clear reference to which character is chosen? • Does the writer support the description with illustrations/quotations from the book? • Does the writer give reasons for his/her choice?	• Does the writer use a fairly informal style with a personal tone? • Is the text in a suitable format?
Range and accuracy of structures and vocabulary	**Effect on the reader**
• Do the errors interfere with understanding the ideas? • Does the writer use a variety of sentence structures? • Does the writer use a range of vocabulary?	• Would the reader be able to understand the character from the description without reading the book? • Would the reader clearly understand the writer's reasons for choosing the character? • Is the answer suitable for a college student to read?
Organisation	
• Are the main ideas separated into paragraphs? • Does the writer use linking words and expressions to make the text easy to follow?	

8 Edit your text

a Look back at the text in **7 Be your own examiner** and make the following changes.

1 Look at this sentence from the introduction.

Sometimes we hate him, and other times we feel sorry for him.

Does the writer put the reasons for hating Heathcliff and for pitying him into separate paragraphs? Make an outline for the text, organising the reasons into appropriate paragraphs and making notes for an introduction and conclusion.

2 Does the writer clearly state reasons for choosing Heathcliff? Indicate where reasons could go on the outline you made in **1**.

3 Underline any parts of the answer that are irrelevant.

4 Correct the underlined words in the text.

5 Find all the instances of *and* in the model text. How many times did the writer use this word? Use different connecting words in as many places as is appropriate.

6 Replace *bad* (line 5 twice) and *badly* (line 14) with more specific, accurate words.

b Do one of the following activities.

1 If you have read *Wuthering Heights*, rewrite the model text, making the changes listed in **a**.

2 If you haven't read *Wuthering Heights*, write an answer on the book or story of your choice, using the changes in **a** to help you.

Exam practice: Write a composition

You are going to write a composition on the topic below. Do the tasks which follow.

> Imagine that a film is being made of the book you have read. Which role would you like to play? Say which character you would most like to be and why.

Write your **composition** (120–180 words).

• **Read the question**

Read the question and underline the key points. Check you know which type of answer to write (story, article, etc.).

• **Think about your reader**

Identify your reader, and a suitable style.

• **Make a plan**

Make an outline for your answer.

• **Think about content**

Write your answer, using descriptive expressions to portray your character, and adding examples or quotations from the book to support your description.

• **Edit your text**

Check your writing for errors when you have finished.

Further practice

Write a story on the topic below.

> What do you think happened to the characters after the end of the book? Write a short story about one of the main or minor characters in the book you have read.

Write your short **story** (120–180 words).

Writing Bank

Informal letters

Greeting and endings

Dear (Sally), ... love/best wishes/regards, (Jack)

Introductions

How are you?

I'm sorry I haven't written for so long/ages, but ...
(give reason).

It's been a long time since I last heard from you.

I thought I'd drop you a line to see how you are
getting on.

As I haven't heard from you for ages, I thought I'd
write to see how you are.

Thanks for your letter. It was interesting/good to hear
that ... (give example).

I got your letter yesterday, and decided to write back
straightaway.

Thank you for writing such a long and funny letter.
I always enjoy reading what you've been doing.

Conclusions

Well, that's all my news. Write back soon, telling me
what you've been up to.

Please write to me again soon, and tell me all
your news.

Please give my regards to (your parents). Hope to hear
from you soon.

That's about all from me. What about you? Write back
soon, telling me what you've been doing recently.

Give (Peter) my regards if you see (him), and tell (him)
to drop me a line.

Say hello to (Ana) from me.

I'm looking forward to your next letter, so
write soon!

I can't wait to hear (how you did in your exams),
so write as soon as you know!

Giving advice

Why don't you ...?

If I were you, I'd ...

Have you thought of ...ing?

I would recommend ...

My advice is to ...

It would be a good idea to ...

You should/shouldn't ...

Don't forget to ...

Describing objects

Order of adjectives

- The general rule for the order of adjectives is:
  (1) general description or opinion words, (2) size, (3)
  age, (4) colour, (5) origin + NOUN + *with* (features).

- We do not normally write more than three adjectives
  before the noun, e.g. *We have a comfortable, large,
  blue Ford with electric windows and air-conditioning.*
- When you write more than one adjective before
  a noun, do not write *and*. Put a comma after each
  adjective except for the last one. Do not use long
  lists of adjectives to describe the same noun.

Formal letters

Letters of application

Greetings and endings

Name of addressee not known:
   Dear Sir/Madam, ... Yours faithfully, (John Vernon)

Name of addressee known:
   Dear (Mr White), ... Yours sincerely, (John Vernon)

Introductions

I am writing to (apply for/enquire about, etc.) ..., which
was advertised in ...

With reference to your advertisement, I am writing to .../
I am interested in ...

I am writing in connection with your advertisement in
(*The Times*) ...

Useful phrases

I would like the opportunity to ...

I would say that I am ...

I would be interested in ...

As you can see from my CV, I ...

I have had a great deal of experience in ...

Although I do not have a lot of experience in this field,
I feel that I can ...

Concluding

I enclose my CV and the names of two referees.

I can be contacted at the above address.

Please do not hesitate to contact me if you require
further information.

I hope to hear from you soon.

I look forward to your reply.

I look forward to hearing from you soon.

Making a request

Thanking

Thank you for your ...

Thank you for ...ing

I am very grateful for your ...

You were very (kind/helpful/hospitable, etc.) while
I was in England, for which I am very grateful.

I am writing to thank you very much for ...

I really appreciated your ...

I would like to thank you for ...

Requesting

Could you please ...?
I wonder if you could ...?
I wonder if it is at all possible for you to ...?
I would be very grateful if you would/could ...
Would it be possible (for you) to ...?
I would greatly appreciate it if you could/would ...

Letters to the editor

Introductions

I have just read a letter in (your magazine) about ...
I am writing to express my opinion about a letter
published in your (newspaper).
With reference to the letter about ..., published
in your (newspaper), I am writing to say that
I agree/disagree with the idea that ...

Conclusions

I wonder if any of your readers agree with me?
I am sure that many readers will support my idea.
Do any more readers feel the same way?

Expressing opinions

I am of the opinion that ...
It seems to me that ...
As far as I am concerned, ...
In my opinion, ...
I believe/think/support the idea that ...
I am (strongly) in favour of ...
I couldn't agree more that ...
I am firmly opposed to the idea that ...
I am totally against the idea that ...
It is a shame/disgusting/terrible that ...

Transactional letters

Writing tips

- Remember to include all the keys points as set out in the question.
- Try to avoid copying directly from the question. If you can think of other ways to express the keys points in the question, you will get credit for this.
- When a question gives a lot of details (e.g. a timetable), try and summarise this information.
- Think carefully about what you want your letter to achieve and what effect you want it to have on the reader. Remember to use the correct tenses and verbs forms for the purpose of your letter.

Asking for information

Introductions

I am writing to enquire about ...
I would like some more information about ...
I would like to enquire about ...
I would be grateful if you could give me some
information about ...

Conclusions

Thanking you for your help in this matter.
I look forward to hearing from you.
I look forward to receiving your reply.
I look forward to your reply.
I would be grateful if you could send me this
information as soon as possible.
I would be grateful for an early reply to my enquiries.
I hope to hear from you soon.

Asking for information

I would like to know if/where/what, etc. ...
I would be grateful if you could tell me ...
Could you tell me ...?

Giving information

Introductions

I am writing to let you know about ...
I have managed to get some information about ...
I am writing to tell you the possibilities for ...

Conclusions

Write back and let me know what you think is best.
Write and tell me your decision.
Write back and let me know what you have decided.

Making arrangements

Introductions

(See also *Thanking* in **Making a request** on p.124.)
I am pleased that you have accepted our invitation.
I am writing to let you know what arrangements have
been made for your (visit).
I am writing to let you know the plans for your (visit).
I am writing to give you details of your planned (visit) to ...
I wanted to inform you of the arrangements that have
been made for ...

Conclusions

If you should need/require any further information,
please do not hesitate to contact me.
I will contact you to confirm/finalise our arrangements.
I can be contacted at ..., if you need to get in touch.
Please call me if you need any help.
We are all looking forward to ... on the (4th December).

Making arrangements

Useful phrases

(See also **Asking for information** and **Giving information** on p.125.)

We have arranged for you to …

The arrangements for the … have been finalised.

Making a complaint

Introductions

I am writing to complain about …

I am writing in connection with …, which I saw advertised …

I have to say that I was not at all satisfied with …

I am sorry to say that I was extremely disappointed with …

I am afraid to say that I have a number of complaints about …

Conclusions

I am sure that you will understand that I was very (disappointed/dissatisfied, etc.) with …

I would like to hear your explanation for this.

I would like you to investigate this matter, and let me know your decision.

I would like a complete refund as soon as possible.

I would like a full or partial refund.

I would like to have all of my money refunded.

Could you please make arrangements to refund all my money?

Could you please arrange for me to receive a new (radio/CD, etc.) or refund my money in full?

Stories

Writing tips

- Give just a little interesting information in your introduction to make the reader want to read on.
- Don't give away the details of the events in the first paragraph.
- Use a range of past tenses in your story.
- Try to use specific vocabulary to describe events and people. Avoid 'general' words like *good*, *bad*, etc.
- Try to include some direct speech in your story to make it more dramatic. Use a range of verbs to introduce direct speech.
- If you use direct speech, use the correct punctuation.

Discursive compositions

Writing tips

- Decide what kind of discursive composition is required before you start to write:
- discussing pros and cons in which you write a balanced argument.
- giving your personal opinion. This may be a balanced argument if you have no strong opinion.
- suggesting solutions in which you make suggestions about a problem.
- State your position on the topic in the introduction, according to the type of composition required. In a balanced argument, write a general introductory paragraph, stating the two contrasting ideas.
- In a balanced argument, use two main paragraphs: one discussing the points for, and one discussing the points against. Use a topic sentence in each paragraph, and back it up by adding two or three supporting details.
- In a balanced argument, write a summarising sentence in your conclusion, perhaps giving your personal opinion.
- Make your argument explicit and specific by adding examples or illustrations of your main point.

Useful language

(See also **Expressing opinions** on p.125.)

I couldn't agree/disagree more with the statement.

I agree with the statement up to a point.

I agree with the statement to a certain extent.

I cannot see one point in favour of the statement.

It is clear that there are two sides to this argument.

Reports

Writing tips

- Reports need to be set out clearly to make the information in them as accessible as possible. There is more than one way to set out a report, but the following guidelines and template on p.127 give you one standard way. (See also pp.94 and 98.)
- Use headings at the top of the report to clearly highlight key information.
- Use main headings for the introduction and conclusion and to separate the main points. (These replace topic sentences used in other types of writing.) Possible headings for the main points include *General information, Facilities, Suitability for …, Positive points, Negative points*, etc.
- For the details under each heading, you can use numbered points.
- Always use a formal style of writing.

```
REPORT
To:
From:
Date:
Subject:
Introduction

Main heading
1
2
Main heading
1
2
Main heading
1
2
etc.
Conclusion
```

Evaluating places

Introductions

As requested, I have (visited) the (Hotel Miramar), in order to (assess the suitability) of (state the purpose of the report from the question).

As requested, this report is to … (state purpose).

The purpose of this report is to … (state purpose), as requested.

Conclusions

In spite of the disadvantages, I would strongly recommend …

Although there are certain drawbacks, I would recommend …

There are no obvious disadvantages; therefore, I would highly recommend …

The drawbacks outweigh the advantages, so I would not recommend …

The positive aspects of … make it highly suitable for …

The drawbacks of … make it unsuitable for …

I have no hesitation in recommending the …

I have certain reservations about …, but, overall, it is a … for …

Evaluating proposals

Writing tips

- Headings for a typical report of this kind could be
  Introduction, Sports Stadium, Theatre, Conclusion/Recommendation

Useful language

- Note the punctuation (:) used in the following phrases, to indicate that a list of points follows.

  This would benefit (the town) in many ways:
  This would offer the following advantages:
  This would provide the following benefits:
  The main reasons in favour of this proposal are:

Conclusions

While (state proposal) would …, the (state other proposal) would …

In my opinion, the best proposal is …, because …

The (state proposal) would clearly offer far greater benefits to …, and it is my recommendation that …

The (state proposal) clearly would create more problems than it solves, so it is my recommendation that (state other proposal) …

Articles

Writing tips

- Articles can be on almost any topic, and have any reader. It is therefore important to think about your reader and choose an appropriate style.

- Your article will be published in a magazine or newspaper of some kind, or perhaps included in a book of articles, like an anthology. Think about who might read such a publication, in order to select an appropriate style of writing. When the reader could be just about anybody, think about one possible reader, and write for that reader.

- Remember that reviews will include recommendations. Decide on your opinion of the film or book, etc. that you are reviewing, and show this opinion in your recommendations.

- It is a good technique to directly address your readers in articles. Imagine that you are 'speaking' to them through your article. To involve your reader, ask questions, give advice, give encouragement where appropriate, persuade, suggest, etc.

- You can also illustrate your articles with your own personal experience, by telling stories or describing your own experiences.

Linking devices

Relative clauses

- You can join two ideas together with a relative clause. Use a relative pronoun to start the second clause.

- The relative pronouns are: *which/that* (for things); *who/whom/that* (for people), and *where* (for places).

- A relative pronoun can refer back to one word, a phrase, or to a whole clause.

Connectors

Note:

- Some connectors are shown as appearing in the middle of a sentence, after a comma. These words and phrases can also be used at the beginning of a sentence in the first clause. The word or first word of the phrase should be written with a capital letter.
- Some connectors are shown with a capital letter on the word or first word of the phrase. These must be used to begin a new sentence.

Reason

..., because ...
..., as ...
..., since ...
..., for ...
..., due to ...
..., because of ...
One/Another reason for ... is ...

Result

..., so ...
..., so that ...
As a result, ...
Consequently, ...
Therefore, ...
Thus, ...
This, in turn, produces/causes ...
One/Another effect/result is ...
This means that ...

Showing the sequence of ideas

Firstly,... / First of all, ... / In the first place, ...
Furthermore, ... / In addition, ... / Another point/
   effect is ...
Finally, ... / Lastly, ... / A final point is ...
In conclusion, ... / To conclude, ...

Note: *At last*

Do not use *At last* to show the sequence of ideas. Use this phrase only in narratives.

Introducing options

First of all, ...

The first	option	is ...
A second	way	
Another	choice	
The last	possibility	
The final		

Contrast

..., but ...
..., even though ...
..., despite ...
..., in spite of ...
..., although ...
However, ...
On the other hand, ...
On the contrary, ...
Nevertheless, ...

Note: *In spite of/Despite* and *Although*

- *In spite of* and *despite* are prepositions, and must be followed by a noun phrase, e.g. *In spite of/Despite **the strike**, our plane took off on time.* Despite is not followed by *of.*
- ***Although*** is a connector and must be followed by a verb phrase.
  e.g. *Although **there was** a strike, our plane took off on time.*

Addition

..., and ...
To make matters worse, ...
In addition, ...
Furthermore, ...
Moreover, ...
Another point/effect/result is ...
Equally important is ...

Useful connectors in stories

Start of the story

The first thing that happened was ...
In the beginning, ...

Following parts of the story

Then, ...
Later, ... / Later on, ...
After some time, ...
A little while later, ...
After that, ...
The next thing ...

Events that happened fast/slowly

Suddenly, ...
All of a sudden, ...
In an instant, ...
Immediately, ...
Gradually, ...
Slowly, ...

Events in the future of the story

Soon, ...
In a few minutes, ...
In the next few hours, ...

The end of the story

Finally, ...
At last, ...
Eventually, ...

Note: *At last/Eventually*

These indicate that the final event happened after difficulty, or after a long time.

Giving examples/illustrating

..., such as ...
..., like ...
For example, ...
For instance, ...
One/Another example of ... is ...
In particular, ...
To be specific, ...